LAUNCH *your* VISION

*A Strategic Guide
for Visionaries, Artists,
and Kingdom Builders*

REBECCA FRIEDLANDER

Contents

INTRODUCTION

Many artists begin their journey like lovers waiting to be pursued. Our hearts are eager yet shy, waiting for someone to help us spread our wings – a fairy godmother to make us spectacular with just a flick of her wand, or the Simon Cowell to pick us out from the crowd and give us a platform. We might not admit it, but most of us think that having someone "discover us" would make our creative lives a lot easier. We feel the stirring... we know God has placed a hunger for artistic expression in our lives, and we desire to use our gifts to honor Him.

"If it's God's will," we declare with certainty, "He will make it happen."

We may even believe that a sovereign act of God would prove a higher power to be solely responsible for the opportunity, rather than our own flesh or prideful ambition accomplishing our dreams. *If God does it*, we reason, *I can't mess it up*. The heart behind this idea has merit, but the problem is that God doesn't always work that way. In fact, He rarely does, since He doesn't honor fear (even when we're afraid of ourselves) but rather, He honors faith and obedience. The result is that there are many disillusioned visionary people who are waiting in the wings and never step into their creative destiny.

For many years, I was one of those people. I had some amount of natural talent and a passion to serve God with my gifts, but I was clueless when it came to unlocking my dreams. For many years I hoped and prayed for the "big break" which never happened. I became frustrated with life and even somewhat mad at God, because I couldn't figure out why He put such a burning, artistic zeal in my heart and didn't give me the outlet to use it.

Like Joseph in the Old Testament, I had a lot of big dreams that seemed overwhelming to everyone around me, and I didn't know what to do with them. I resonated with this young dreamer who carried great favor, but that mostly served to make others jealous. Joseph was a remarkable man; eventually he cracked the code of how to unlock a dream and see it happen. He went from being a dreamer to becoming an interpreter of dreams, and after creating a track record of faithfulness, he could hear a king's vision and create the strategy to bring it to pass. **Because of this process, Joseph went from a dreamer with no following to a strategic visionary who saved a nation.**

After 17 years of ministry as a full-time artist, I'd like to offer you some coaching on how to partner with God to

6

launch your dreams. By the end of this book, you'll know how to craft a strategy to build your vision and sharpen your faith until you can throw your head back and laugh at your fears. Instead of causing people to be intimidated or jealous of your dreams, I believe you can use God's favor on your life to fulfill your destiny. I'd love to see you discover the joy of creating with your Father in unpredictable, never-before-seen, radical ways that introduce heaven to earth and captivate the human heart.

As believers in Christ carrying the divine mandate to "be fruitful," I believe that media, film, art, books, and other creative projects are powerful opportunities that the Lord loves to use to bring this calling to pass. The Lord who placed vision and creativity into your heart did so for a reason, and He wants come alongside your journey to help it unfold, change lives, and bring Him glory!

The nine chapters of coaching within this book carry keys for your journey. Not all of them will be applicable to your personal walk, but some of them may be perfectly shaped to unlock the next phase of your calling. I'll share my personal, three-step strategy on how I take a vision from the "idea stage" to launching it into full flight, and I'll be honest about the times I've stumbled along the way. We'll also look deep into God's Word and study the life of Jesus to see how He built a ministry from scratch in a way that honored the Father and fulfilled His destiny. Through Christ's journey and the lives of other important artists and visionaries in Scripture, we'll find heroes and pioneers to equip us for our walk.

The fact is, I believe God is even more excited about your dreams than you are! If you can place them in His hands like an uncut diamond, and can trust Him in the process of crafting a jewel from your raw hopes and dreams, anything is possible! With a little coaching, you'll be able to craft your own strategy and launch your vision.

PART I

READY:
PREPARING YOUR MIND AND HEART FOR THE CREATIVE PROCESS.

"Give me six hours to chop down a tree and I will spend the first four sharpening the axe."

- Abraham Lincoln

Launch the Vision

CHAPTER ONE
KNOWN

To be known and not loved is our greatest fear.
But to be fully known and truly loved is,
well, a lot like being loved by God.
It is what we need more than anything.

It liberates us from pretense,
humbles us our of our self-righteousness,
and fortifies us for any difficulty life can throw at us.
-- Tim Keller

During my career, I've produced 12 music albums of original songs, TV shows and series, films, docudramas, traveled around the world with my potter's wheel, written books, spoken at churches, schools, and retreats, and always have a few creative projects going! However, my creativity didn't start with a platform, rather, it followed a miserable season of feeling stuck and frustrated with most of my life-- especially my creative journey. Believe me, I know what it feels like to think the whole world couldn't care less about your vision. I've also discovered the absolute joy of watching people come alive and be touched through encountering the art that I've partnered with God to birth into the earth. Moments like that simply cannot be put into words! It was quite a trek toward this discovery, but I believe the transition started in Deadwood, TX where I did what many of us do when we feel at our wit's end: I gave up on my dreams.

DEADWOOD

Ever since I was six-years-old, I'd wanted to write music and be a recording artist. It was my life's goal, I'd written hundreds of songs, learned to play the guitar and piano, and went to dozens of music concerts to hang on every word of my heroes. I couldn't imagine loving anything more than music. It was more than a desire – it was part of my heart. Music was a gift from God, and I knew it. I also knew it was way bigger than I could make possible on my own, and the frustration of hoping for something that wasn't happening was maddening.

In my early twenties, I was still living at home when my family moved to Deadwood, TX: "no man's land" with a hand-painted sign on the highway that read, *Welcome to Deadwood. Population 100: 99 happy people and one old grouch.* (The residents said they all took turns being the grouch.) We moved there to start a ministry, but the whole thing fell apart when we arrived. In fact, the doors closed so firmly that it was laughable! Living on the banks of the muddy Sabine River at the end of a three-mile dirt road didn't leave much hope for a creative platform, since there wasn't any chance of being discovered in Deadwood. In frustration, I finally told God, *I'm tired of hurting because I want this so badly. If You don't want me to sing, then please tell me what you DO have for my life!*

When I hit a wall in Deadwood, it was crushing. Musical expression lost all it's joy, so I decided to lay it aside to seek God's plan, and for the next year I didn't play a note. I fasted and prayed, and set up my potter's wheel in the little shed with a cracked cement floor, listened to worship music, formed clay pots, and got quiet before God. Something interesting started happening: I began to think of the beauty in the scriptural parable of the Potter & Clay, and I wrote my thoughts down. My heart started coming alive with this new medium of art: writing.

God started showing up in Deadwood. In my quiet times of prayer, I began to sense His Presence so strongly as He healed my heart, revealed some idols I'd been holding onto, and visited me in a way that I had always longed for but had never fully experienced. He challenged me with the price tag involved in receiving the anointing, and asked me if I was sure if I wanted it. (I had grown up in a Christian home but no one had ever told me about "anointing," so this was totally new for me.) I knew He was offering me an option to step into a ministry that was far better than anything I could conjure up on my own, and I was enthralled (and terrified) of this beautiful idea.

At the end of a year, a Methodist minister from Deadwood approached me.

"The Lord says that it's time for you to start your ministry," he said, gently but with certainty, "and it's going to start in my church. Bring your potter's wheel and speak to our ladies."

He had been praying for revival for 30 years, and he noticed that God was up to something with me! So, I lugged my huge wheel to the Methodist ladies' meeting and have been speaking ever since. After almost two years, I moved from Deadwood to a larger town and spent 2 ½ years interning at a recording studio run by a pastor and his wife, rethinking my definition of music and how that fit into my life. They challenged me to grow and pursue my calling and gifts with passion, and I came out of that season understanding how to honor authority and serve someone else's vision. I never went to college. Eventually I picked up a camera and started filming and editing my own TV shows for a local TV station. The "death of vision" in Deadwood became a powerful place to launch my dreams, because that's where God showed up. That's how my ministry and arts career started, and it embedded a few valuable keys into my soul.

DREAMING WITH GOD

Deadwood wrecked me. I realized that God *wanted me* more than He wanted my dreams. His love for me was bigger than any "destiny" or anything that I wanted to do for Him, and I didn't have to force His hand with any of it.

He wanted me to create, in fact He had more ideas than I did! He also called even more artistic mediums out of me – I thought I just wanted to sing, but by the end of that season I had written and illustrated four books. (I didn't even know how to draw before then!) He bypassed the way I limited my gifts and decided to color outside of my lines. The wrecking ball of His Presence was glorious, and I was hooked: partnering with God to create beauty was what I was born to do.

The biggest thing that still wrecks me is that *He knows us so deeply.* This fills that artist's cry in my soul to be known and cheered on. Many of us have been told that this longing to be known is evil or self-centered. Truthfully, and if pursued in the wrong way, it can be very damaging and we miss the greatest goals. However, if we recognize that God wants to reach inside of us and release creative gifts we didn't even know we had, and that we get to be part of His Kingdom which is so much bigger than ourselves, we'd do everything possible to position ourselves in such a way to give Him all we're holding back.

If we can recognize that God is already holding out His hand and waiting to pull us into the dance... if we can see the delight and longing in His eyes as He desires to partner with us, we'll find the One who is willing to whisk us onto the dance floor and take us into an incredible journey.

THE FATHER'S BLESSING

If we look at the ministry of Jesus, we'll notice a trend of the Father's love that's very different than a normal ministry or career lifestyle. In my own mind, I can imagine the Father hoping that Christ would accomplish His assignment on earth and throwing a party when He did, but that's not what we see. The first benediction of the Father's pleasure came prior to any ministry at all. In fact, the Father's approval was stamped upon the Son before He called any disciples, did a single miracle, went to the cross, or rose from the dead.

When Jesus was thirty-years-old, local people knew Him as the carpenter from Nazareth. Then one day, He laid down the hammer and chisel and hiked into the wilderness to see His cousin, John the Baptist, who was leading a radical revival by the Jordan river. People were confessing their sins and being baptized in droves, and the masses were eagerly looking for the chosen Messiah who would bring freedom to their nation.

Standing in the river, his piercing eyes cutting through the crowds, John saw Jesus standing on the bank.

"Look!" John shouted with triumph. "This is the one I told you about: behold the Lamb of God!"

Jesus stepped into the water towards John, but his cousin nearly refused to baptize him.

"I should be the one being baptized by you," he whispered hoarsely, as the people looked on in wonder.

"Do it," said Jesus, "it needs to happen in order to fulfill God's plan."

Suddenly the heavens opened, the Holy Spirit descended like a dove, and Father God's voice released a blessing upon His son:

This is My beloved Son, in whom I am well pleased!

Nobody knew who Jesus was or supposed that He was anything other than a carpenter, yet the Father, beaming from heaven, opened the skies and shouted, *I love you, My Son! I am so pleased with You!*

For the rest of His ministry, we never see Jesus trying to earn the Father's approval or impress Him with good deeds. Instead, He worked from the place of blessing and acceptance, knowing that He had been heard, was tracking with the Father's plan, and trusting that His Father had the details covered. He never denies the desire to be known and loved, but rather He gives us the picture of someone who fully tapped into the heart of God and lives from the place of complete trust in His Father's love.

Like Jesus, when you live "from the place of blessing" in your creative journey, you never have to ask God to prove His love by opening doors or releasing resources. Instead, you're confident in His love, you know that His dreams are bigger than yours, and He's already provided everything you need for the vision. Your creativity is not birthed from the place of a needy orphan, but as a beloved child of the Father who is present and ready to walk every step with you.

I remember one moment early in my creative journey that revealed the Father's blessing in a way that made my jaw drop in amazement...

HE KNOWS YOUR NAME

Crowds buzzed with anticipation and the atmosphere was charged with excitement over the evening's concert. Several internationally recognized bands were playing that evening, and the fans were ready to give them a Texas welcome. As a reporter for a small local newspaper, I drove my little Toyota SUV behind the event center and somehow managed to slip behind security guards as I hoped for a fresh scoop. All my life, I'd listened to these bands on my little FM radio, taping their posters to my bedroom walls and memorizing their song lyrics. The newspaper had given me the job of covering local events and helped open doors to interview some of my heroes. There was only one problem: they hadn't given me a press pass yet, so I hoped my job title alone would get me into a few interviews with the lead singers. It was a bit ambitious, but a local radio station had promised to help and I figured I had nothing to lose. It turned out to be an unforgettable evening that would reveal how God believed in my dreams even more than I did, and He knew right where I was!

With a pounding heart, I approached the road manager and placed my request for an interview, using my nicest smile and sharing the name of the local paper that had sent me.

"We'll see," he said, warily disappearing into his trailer.

Soon the security officer got wind that an annoying blonde woman was asking for interviews, and he came out with a scowl.

"This isn't a good time. How did you get back here anyway?" he demanded, ready to bid me a speedy farewell. I gulped and scrambled for words.

Suddenly a man interrupted our conversation.

"Excuse me, are you..." he pulled a piece of paper from his shirt pocket with my name scribbled on the top, "Rebecca Friedlander? I'm from the radio station and I can set up a few interviews for you."

A little shiver of delight shot through me. *Perfect timing!* I thought. *God knows right where I am, and He sent someone who has my name in his pocket to create a way for me.*

I don't remember a single thing that my heroes said during the interviews that night, but I do remember feeling loved and known by my Heavenly Father who showed up at just the right moment. His blessing had gone before me to prepare the way, and He knew my name.

KNOWN BY GOD

The fact that a disc jockey could have the name of a random reporter in his shirt pocket is a great reminder of God's heart: we are known, our dreams are not despised, we are called to walk with a very creative God who shows up right on time. This idea of being deeply seen and known by God is key to the creative journey. Artists and ministers are often bombarded by insecurities, accusations, and over-analyzing, but the pressure lifts when we are deeply rooted in the Father's love. Suddenly, our identity isn't wrapped up in our dreams when we realize we are already loved and cherished by Christ.

As we follow the life of Jesus, we see that His identity and emotional stability never depended on whether it looked like His ministry was successful, but only on whether He was following the Father. When faced with pressures or difficulties, He always retreated to prayer where He could center Himself around the most important thing: His Father's love, companionship, and plan. Being known in heaven by His Father was more important to Jesus than anything on earth.

When the disciples were flying high after a successful ministry trip, He cheered them on and then counseled,

Nevertheless do not rejoice in this...
but rather rejoice because your names are written in heaven.
Luke 10:20

When our names are known in heaven, it is more glorious than any earthly reward and will keep us focused on what really matters, regardless of what happens on this earth. Great ministry platforms come and go, but being deeply rooted in the place of heavenly identity provides great security.

Jesus also laments the lack of knowing Him deeply. It would seem that He longs for us to enter into this space of love and intimacy, and some doors are shut simply because we have not embraced this place. To the five virgins who were late to the wedding, He refused them access to the wedding party with the words,

Assuredly I say unto You, I do not know you.
Matthew 25: 12

In the Old Testament, the prophets became so burdened by the heart of the Lord, that their lament echoes through the ages as they pen the heart cry of God, *My people have not known Me!*

Could it be that our desire to "be known" as artists and visionaries, stems from an even deeper, God-given desire to be deeply known by Him? Our wish for a Simon Cowell to acknowledge us as the next American Idol and help launch our dreams may actually be a guise for a deep-seated yearning to be known and affirmed by the true Creator who can launch our vision for greater purposes than our own.

Thankfully, this is something Christ freely gives us. He doesn't hold out on us, but rather waits to see if we are really serious about pursuing this intimacy. Like a careful lover, He does not easily share His heart with just everyone. Instead, He waits to see if we will also invest in this relationship before entrusting us with His creative treasures.

KNOWN IN HEAVEN

When we connect with our Father's love, the fact that we're known in heaven seems to make room for us on earth. Here's another story when I found this to be true in the creative process.

❧

It was summertime in Northern Israel, and I was following a very tentative lead on a story. When traveling alone with a backpack of cameras to film my TV show, *Radical Makeovers*, I checked into a youth hostel which happened to be next door to the local zoo where I could watch the tigers prowling below and listen to the peacocks scream from my bedroom. It was quite an adventure!

Weeks earlier I had emailed the Christian leader of a congregation and asked if she knew anyone I might interview. She had been one of my heroes, and I'd listened to her beautiful music for years in my little studio at home. No reply had come from my email, so I simply decided to visit her fellowship and thank her for her ministry.

Crammed into a car with several people going to worship, we drove the winding, mountain roads to the beautiful building. After the moving worship service, I put on my brave face and made a beeline to speak with her.

"Thanks so much for all you do," I offered. "Your music has encouraged me so much!"

"Tell me why you're in Israel," she countered graciously, so I shared my heart for young women and the passion that had birthed this TV show about capturing true beauty around the world. She quickly interrupted me.

"You sent us an e-mail! We didn't get the chance to respond, but we know who you are. Come have lunch with us!"

Soon I was seated at the head table (next to my hero!) in a cafe, eating a banquet of rich Mediterranean food and talking about potential connections for my show. The networking was invaluable and many people were touched by the interview that came from that time, but my heart will never forget the feeling of being "known" by God in a foreign country as I stepped out to pursue my vision. I was a "nobody," just a camera girl with a dream, but God knew where I was and spread me a feast when I least expected it.

This place of "knowing" has become the most sacred space of my life. It's the heartbeat of everything I do as an artist and a human being. If I get distracted from this place, I often try to meet peoples' needs in the wrong way or miss out on a beautiful moment He has prepared for me to walk with Him in. God gives talent and anointing to lots of people: but I want to know Him deeply enough to catch the rhythm of His heart and share it with the world using my art.

Partnering with God starts with this place of being known by the Father. The Apostle John wrote to those who were new in the faith and said,

> *I write to you, little children,*
> *Because you have known the Father.*
> 1 John 2:13

The more we know the Father, the more we get to be little children who rest in His love. The pressure lifts, and we get to enjoy the process without trying to prove ourselves to the world.

A STRONG FOUNDATION

Built around the affirmation of God, our hearts can thrive in the safety of His love even when others may or may not understand or value our contribution. Having the strong foundation of His love in our lives enables us to overcome the words that might unintentionally undermine our dreams.

One time I was releasing a film at a church (I had invested major blood, sweat, and tears into this project!), and I overheard two ladies talking in the restroom.

"Sally was going to come," one lady said, "but she saw the film trailer and decided she wasn't interested in the topic, so she changed her mind."

For a moment, the sharp stab of rejection made me wince. In response, I quickly stepped back into the "known" place and remembered, *This is God's film, not mine. I'm just a servant trying to give Him my best, and the results are up to Him.* Wryly, I thought to myself, *The devil must be pretty mad to try to discourage me right before the film starts!* If I had become focused on defending myself, it could have ruined my evening. Instead, I shifted into the "known" place where I simply give God my best, rest in His love, and trust Him to work out the details. It turned out to be a great night!

Jesus modeled this for us at The Last Supper, revealing how to stay focused on being "known" by God even in the midst of difficulty. On the night He was betrayed, He could have tried to talk the disciples into following Him to the end, reminded them not to forget His teachings, or had Judas gagged and tied so the betrayal would have never taken place! Instead, His focus was not on defending a ministry or saving a platform: He was completely centered on the Father and serving the disciples with love.

Jesus, knowing that the Father
had given all things into His hands,
and that He had come from God and was going to God,
rose from supper and laid aside His garments,
took a towel and girded Himself.

After that, He poured water into a basin and began to wash the
disciples' feet,
and to wipe them with the towel with which He was girded.
John 13:3-5

Jesus was so wrapped up in knowing what the Father had given Him, that not even His own death could deter Him. He could have tried to talk the disciples into being faithful or boosted His own self-confidence, but He did none of those things. In fact, He embraced the humble, vulnerable state of stripping His outer garments and washing feet. What an awesome place of complete fearlessness! The reason for this is summed up in John's words: *Jesus, **knowing** that the Father had given all things* *into His hands*—His confidence and love flowed from the place of knowing, and He invites us into the same place today.

For an artist, it's so crucial that we experience this intimacy with the Father, since we often naturally tend to live from the heart. Who else puts their heart on the line as much as someone who dares to express it through art and ministry? The deeper we go into the beauty of knowing the love of Christ, the more confidently we can express the dreams and visions He entrusts us with. Cultivating this place of intimacy is a great way to start the creative journey as we launch our vision!

ASK YOURSELF:

1. Do you ever feel frustrated with the creative process?

_____

_____

_____

_____

_____

_____

_____

2. Have you ever been through a "Deadwood" season?

_____

_____

_____

_____

_____

_____

_____

3. How does Christ make us look more like Himself in "Deadwood?"

_____

_____

_____

_____

_____

_____

_____

4. What character attributes are formed during this time?

_____

_____

_____

_____

_____

_____

_____

5 Are you inviting God into your creative journey?

_____

_____

_____

_____

_____

_____

6 What does that look like?

_____

_____

_____

_____

_____

_____

7 Does deeply knowing Christ help center your artistic journey? Explain?

_____

_____

_____

_____

_____

_____

8 What would it look like to spend a season really pressing into God's heart?

_____

_____

_____

_____

_____

_____

9 What are some ways you have experienced Christ's love?

_____

_____

_____

_____

_____

_____

10 List a few ways you can continue to invest in your relationship with Him during the artistic process.

_____

_____

_____

_____

_____

_____

_____

CHAPTER TWO

UN-STUCK

Fear is the glue that keeps us stuck.
Faith is the solvent that sets you free.
- Shannon L. Alder

Have you ever felt stuck in time with your vision? Now more than ever, we have the tools, technology, and resources to make our dreams happen, and with a bit of creativity most people are able to take steps toward their goals – so what keeps us from running with our dreams? I'm going to be radically honest with you in this chapter, because I believe WE are often the ones who hold us back. For years, I was frustrated with God for not making my dreams come true, but now I realize that I was believing so many lies that kept me from giving myself permission to fly. By believing a warped perspective, I was actually clipping my own wings, keeping my vision grounded, and

31

unable to partner with God.

I want to spare you that frustration and prepare you to launch well, so let's look at a few of the common thought-processes that often derail our dreams. Honestly, every one of these lies I've believed myself and often thought they were pleasing to God. Others were spoken by people that I trusted who often had good intentions, but they were simply wrong. So, let's gather our courage, get ready to do a bit of soul-searching, and ask the Lord if there's any wrong beliefs that could keep us stuck in time instead of running after the vision He has given us.

LIE: FALSE HUMILITY

How many of you have "held back" in your creative gifts because you don't want to appear "full of yourself" or prideful? I sure have! My first creative passion was music, but I sang with a very soft voice and was careful not to put too many licks into my vocals. People in my life told me,

"Be careful that you don't sound too worldly. Be humble and don't draw attention to yourself."

Enter the Jacksons, an African American couple who took me under their wing and mentored me at their recording studio right after I left Deadwood. In characteristic candor, they challenged me one day.

"Rebecca, how does it honor God if you give Him less than everything He has placed inside of you?"

I was shocked.

"I never thought I was cheating God by holding myself

back," I responded. "I thought I was being humble."
Suddenly I realized my mistake: by singing softly, I had embraced a false humility and was actually not pleasing God at all. *Lord, I prayed, forgive me for this wrong belief! I want to give You everything!* Their words released a key to a treasure chest that I'd been carrying but was too afraid to open. From that point on, joy flowed over me as I sang to the Lord with every bit of uniqueness and passion within my heart!

Our "best" is not competition for God, since He made the world and isn't jealous or threatened by His creation. To quote the Olympic runner Eric Littel,

"I believe God made me for a purpose, but He also made me fast! And when I run I feel His pleasure."

When we give ourselves permission to be passionate about our vision because God is worthy of our best, we step into the grace to fully be ourselves and give Him glory. When our motive is pure and we desire to honor Christ with our vision, it frees us from false-humility because He is the one we are doing it for. God loves passion. He's not worried about competing with us. No matter how big our dream, He longs to be the Father who cheers us on and dares us to dream bigger still. Never talk yourself out of giving Him your best!

Whatever you do, work at it with all your heart,
as working for the Lord, not for human masters,
since you know that you will receive an inheritance from the
Lord as a reward.

LAUNCH THE VISION

It is the Lord Christ you are serving.
Colossians 3:23, 24 NIV

The Greek word for *heart* in this passage is, "breath," meaning the very God-breathed part of our being. What if we apply this verse to our creative gifts? There is a reward for honoring Christ if we work at it **with all our heart.** Let's dare to give God everything and invest our heart and soul into the vision He's given us!

Truthfully, when we release ourselves to create with big, broad strokes, we usually realize that we're not quite as good as we think we are! No matter how much natural talent, vision, or anointing we carry, most of the time it's a diamond in the rough that needs polishing. This is where true humility kicks in and we have to choose to enter the learning curve to develop our gifts with excellence. Coaching, tutorials, and mentoring help us reach our goals, so having a humble, teachable heart in those areas is so important. If you want true humility, be willing to give your vision everything you have, and then be teachable and ready to mature with your gifts. Refusing the lie of False Humility opens up the door for True Humility to step in.

LIE: COMPARISON

If you're feeling stuck, it's easy to start comparing yourself with others who seem to have life all together, especially if they're thriving in their vision. I've wrestled with the green-eyed monster of envy more than I'd like to admit. Believe me, envy doesn't go away when we step into God's will for our lives. In fact, sometimes it intensifies as we wonder why doors don't open faster or why some people seem to have more opportunities than we do. There are several scriptures that have helped define this issue for me: the first comes directly from the mouth of Jesus. Let's relive a story from John 21:15-19...

⁓

The beach was quiet and serene as the disciples walked with Jesus in Galilee. It seemed so surreal: only days before, they had watched the horrible crucifixion in Jerusalem, and now they were walking with the resurrected Lord. Still raw with emotion and wonder, they hung on His every word.

After a breakfast of fresh fish on the shore, Jesus called Simon Peter over for a private talk. The disciple John, still a teenager and unwilling to let the Master out of his sight, trailed behind them as they walked.

"Peter," said the Lord, laying the call of ministry on Peter's heart, "Feed my sheep."

As He began to unfold the responsibility and cost of ministry, Peter caught sight of young John tagging behind and eavesdropping on the conversation.

"Lord," Peter blurted out, "What about this man?"

Jesus responded with grace and also a challenge.

"If I want him to remain until I come, what is that to you?" He looked straight into Peter's eyes. "Follow Me."

The Holy Spirit often reminds me of this story when I compare my ministry to others'. *What is that to you, Rebecca? Follow Me!* Each of us are directly accountable to God for our lives, and He gives us talents and skills based on His own will and plan. Who are we to compare them with someone else? Instead of being distracted by what others are or are not doing, let's fix our eyes on Jesus and focus on what He has called us to.

But if you have bitter envy and self-seeking in your hearts,
do not boast and lie against the truth.

This wisdom does not descend from above,
but is earthly, sensual, demonic.

For where envy and self-seeking exist,
confusion and every evil thing are there.
James 4:14-16 [bold added]

Ouch! Not only is envy a work of the flesh and even demonic, it also brings confusion. It's hard to be focused on God's calling when we're looking at everyone else. So many people never step into their God-ordained destiny simply because they're lost in the confusion of comparing themselves to others. It's like living life with cross-eyed vision, never focusing solely on the road ahead. If this sounds familiar, recognize that this is a tactic of the enemy to destroy your faith!

One day I was reading through the book of Isaiah and

came across an amazing verse that helped me see clearly how much God hates comparison and wants to give us His best. It shook me up a little and also overwhelmed me with how passionate He is about this topic. While giving powerful promises to Israel about their destiny, God interrupts a litany of blessings to utter these words:

> *For I, the Lord, love justice:*
> *I hate robbery for burnt offering;*
> *I will direct their work in truth,*
> *And will make with them an everlasting covenant.*
> Isaiah 61:8

In the Old Testament, each family was required to bring or purchase their own sacrificial animal as an offering to God. If someone stole an animal and used it for a burnt offering, this was displeasing to Him. You couldn't worship with an offering that wasn't yours. No stealing was allowed in worship.

What would "robbery for burnt offering" look like in today's culture? Today we don't offer sacrifices of animals, but rather we offer sacrifices of worship and service from the heart. When reading this passage, I thought about the times I wished for a ministry like someone else's, and I realized that this type of envy is something that God will not accept I cannot rob someone's ministry and offer it to God: that's robbery for burnt offering. If I try to copy a ministry like so-and-so's to offer to God, that's robbery. To believe that I have less

37

to offer than someone else is an affront to His justice, because He put uniqueness inside of each of His children that pleases Him well. I must give Him what is my own to offer.

Today we have many people who try to be like someone they admire without discovering what God has placed inside of themselves. If we try to rob others' identity and offer it to God, this does not please Him, in fact the word "hate" in this scripture means: *to hate personally, enemy, foe, odious.* God's not joking about this! Instead, He makes a declaration that centers our hearts on His goodness:

> *I will direct their work in truth,*
> *and will make with them an everlasting covenant.*

God doesn't need you to copy someone's ministry or vision! He wants to guide you and entrust you with His perfect plan. He's so serious about this, that He promises to covenant with you and give you something that lasts forever. This is His heart for you! So let's drop the comparison game of envying others. If we're going to focus on the Father's vision for us, we don't have time to be distracted with comparison! It's time to slay the green-eyed monster: God wants to do something beautiful with YOU!

LIE: YOU CAN ONLY DO ONE THING
How many of you have been told, "Just find one thing and focus on that for your career?" Point being, let's avoid

being a jack of all trades and master of none, right? However, I can't find a single reference to that idea in Scripture! In fact, the greatest heroes and warriors of the Bible carried many different weapons, were multi-talented, and God used them in multiple ways. David was a shepherd, armor bearer, warrior, king, songwriter, and prophet. Paul made tents, wrote books, traveled the world, and preached in the streets. Jesus told stories, healed the sick, cast out demons, discipled followers, and calmed seas. Would we actually tell Jesus,

"Lord, why don't you stick to calming the storms and let someone else to do the rest?"

Or perhaps we could tell David,

"You write great music, so just stick to that!"

These multi-faceted people had fully dedicated themselves to God and allowed Him to empower them with whatever the moment required. For those of us who have a lot of vision and creative energy, I want to release you from the lie that says you have to only pick one thing to do! Today I lead worship, film TV shows, write music, shoot photography, and write books, just to name a few things. God often calls me to one type of communication in order to convey what He is speaking, and sometimes one medium of art reaches the goal better than another. Perhaps after writing a song, I discover I have enough vision to write a book too and create several resources. We dare not limit God in the ways He desires to use us.

In order to avoid the "master of none" plight, I have an inner resolution for myself: *Do everything that's in your heart, as long as you do it with excellence.* If I start getting sloppy and can't release the vision well, I'll put it on hold until I can refine my skill set or get some more revelation. However, just because we're not at the necessary skill level doesn't allow us to brush our vision under the rug and ignore it. We are responsible for everything He entrusts us with!

Also, the media/publishing world is now expecting artists to do more than one thing. Social media has taken the power away from the industry leaders and placed it in the hands of the artists. This is great, but followers still expect artists to feed them the same amount of production as a record label or publishing house would. So now an author doesn't just write a book: she writes a book, pens a blog, hosts a podcast, and stays current on social media. This is a great time to toss aside the "only do one thing" concept, because that idea just doesn't work anymore. You're going to need various skills to launch your vision well.

MANY TALENTS

Jesus gives us a remarkable story that reveals how much we are responsible to use everything He gives us.

For the kingdom of heaven is like a man traveling to a far country, who called his own servants and delivered his goods to them. And to one he gave five talents, to another two, and to another one, to each according to his own ability; and immediately he went on a journey.

Then he who had received the five talents went and traded with them, and made another five talents. And likewise he who had received two gained two more also. But he who had received one went and dug in the ground, and hid his lord's money. After a long time the lord of those servants came and settled accounts with them. So he who had received five talents came and brought five other talents, saying,

"Lord, you delivered to me five talents; look, I have gained five more talents besides them."

His lord said to him,

"Well done, good and faithful servant; you were faithful over a few things, I will make you ruler over many things. Enter into the joy of your lord."

He also who had received two talents came and said,

"Lord, you delivered to me two talents; look, I have gained two more talents besides them."

His lord said to him,

"Well done, good and faithful servant; you have been faithful over a few things, I will make you ruler over many things. Enter into the joy of your lord."

Then he who had received the one talent came and said,

"Lord, I knew you to be a hard man, reaping where you have not sown, and gathering where you have not scattered seed. And I was afraid, and went and hid your talent in the ground. Look, there you have what is yours."

But his lord answered and said to him,

"You wicked and lazy servant, you knew that I reap where I have not sown, and gather where I have not scattered seed. So you ought to have deposited my money with the bankers, and at

my coming I would have received back my own with interest. Therefore take the talent from him, and give it to him who has ten talents. For to everyone who has, more will be given, and he will have abundance; but from him who does not have, even what he has will be taken away. And cast the unprofitable servant into the outer darkness. There will be weeping and gnashing of teeth."

Matthew 25:14-30

Several key points stick out to me in this story. First, the Master (Christ) entrusts certain people with many talents and others with few, but He expects each person to invest them fully and make them grow, no matter how many they have. He also rejoiced in the talents of the ten as much as the multiplied talents of the two. The rebuke was reserved for the man who hid his talent and invested nothing in the process of making it grow. **It doesn't matter how much we have, but rather that we invest it fully.**

Secondly, when the talents were used well, it brought great joy to the Master! Do you realize how much joy you bring the Lord when you act on the dreams He gives you? The most beautiful part of the creative process is when you sense the Lord's joy over what you have done with His gifts. The joy over His children's success is wonderful, and the Lord is massively pleased when we step out in faith and invest well in our vision.

The final point: those who are faithful receive more. I cannot emphasize enough how important this is! God is not looking for super-talented people, because He can hand out talents to anyone He wants to. Those who will be faithful with what they have are always entrusted with more, and this includes talent and creativity. Take it from someone who has no college education, no formal training in film or the arts, but has produced TV shows that have aired on PBS and worldwide networks! The biggest principle of my life has been to be faithful with what I have right in front of me and watch God offer more when I use it well. **It's a Kingdom principal: be faithful with what you have and God will multiply it.**

When I was in Deadwood, I wrote a book about the parable of the potter and clay. After I wrote down all I could think of, I head the whisper of my Father say,

Draw some illustrations to go with it.

In the past, I had attempted some sketches but quickly stuffed them in a folder and hid them in my closet. Pulling out my charcoal pencils that day, I was amazed that I could actually draw some pictures that weren't half bad! Then I heard the same whisper,

Try some water colors.

I went to the craft store and bought some paints and watercolor paper. Soon I was playing with oils, pastels, and other artistic mediums as I illustrated my own book! I was shocked! Until that moment, I had never realized that God gives us more talents when we are faithful to use the ones we have for His purposes. Sometimes He sends people along our paths who add their talents to the mix, but other times He wants to multiply the ones we have.

Today, I write my own scripts for films, create costumes for my actors, and do all my own graphic designs. I realize that's more creative juice than most people are interested in having, but I never dreamed of being able to do all these things. The truth is that God is more interested in birthing the visions He has given us than we are, and the One who gave us the passion to begin with is quite capable of giving us the talent we need to pull it off. Quite the opposite of just "doing one thing:" rather, He expects us to use all – and more – of what He's placed inside of us.

By this My Father is glorified, that you bear much fruit;
so you will be My disciples.
John 15:8

The Father loves when we bear fruit! He is so honored when our vision brings Him glory! He may lead us through a wilderness to sharpen our vision and intimacy with Him, but He is not trying to talk you out of what He has called you to do. So if you feel stuck with your vision, don't lose heart! If any of these lies resonate with you, take responsibility and ask His forgiveness for believing the lies. Let Him remind you of the truth, and focus on the goal of fulfilling all He has given you to do!

ASK YOURSELF:

1) False-humility: have you been holding back from giving God everything?

_____

_____

_____

_____

_____

_____

_____

2) Have you felt the need to tone down your passion because others caution you not to "walk in pride?"

_____

_____

_____

_____

_____

3) As you search your heart, do you feel like their cautions are justified, or that your passion is pure and brings God joy? (When in doubt, ask Him to show you!)

_____

_____

_____

_____

4) Comparison: what are some ways that you've compared yourself to others in the past?

_____

_____

_____

_____

_____

_____

_____

5) Have you doubted God's ability to use you?

_____

_____

_____

_____

_____

_____

_____

6) What do you think God says about that?

_____

_____

_____

_____

_____

_____

_____

7) Have you been told, "Pick one thing to do?" Does that phrase limit you or help you focus?

_____

_____

_____

_____

_____

_____

_____

8) What are some areas you may not feel gifted in, but the Father may be calling you to do in order to bring your vision to pass?

_____

_____

_____

_____

_____

_____

9) Even if you don't have the full picture, what are some areas you can be faithful with what you have been given?

_____

_____

_____

_____

_____

10) Ask God to multiply your gifts as you are faithful to use them!

_____

_____

_____

_____

_____

_____

_____

CHAPTER THREE
WRESTLING WITH THE VISION

I've found that anything worth achieving will always have obstacles in the way and you've got to have that drive and determination to overcome those obstacles on route to whatever it is that you want to accomplish.
– Chuck Norris

"We don't like their sound, and guitar music is on the way out"
—Decca Recording Co. rejecting the Beatles 1962

I believe there are two types of visionaries: those who get rejected and stop dreaming, and those who face disappointment and dream anyway. I meet so many dreamers who have been called by the Lord to do great things, but somewhere along the way they simply gave up on their destiny. Maybe you can relate! Sometimes the visions that are the dearest to us end up being tossed aside, and it takes tenacious faith see what God is doing and partner with Him. But oh, the seeing is beautiful! When we get past the frustration and actually see what He is up to, it makes everything worth it! In this current season of my life, I deal with closed doors and disappointment regularly, but I've discovered some ways to move past it. So, I'd like to share a few keys that can help build your faith as we move forward.

The prophet Samuel was given a direct assignment from God and ran into some closed doors along the way. Some of the "no's" even came from God, while he was in the very center of God's will and stepping out in faith. Instead of becoming disillusioned, he probed a bit deeper and discovered a great treasure with God's fingerprints all over it, and this discovery led to an incredible victory for the Kingdom of God. It's a great reminder to stay true to the vision even when what we see with our eyes may conflict with what God told us.

౿

SAMUEL'S QUEST

The nation of Israel was in turmoil, and both prophets and kings were in the thick of the madness. King Saul was anointed by the Prophet Samuel at God's bidding, but the brave yet foolish king chose to follow the wanderings of his own heart rather than the commandments of God. Towering a head and shoulders above the average height, Saul's natural charisma and stance made him an obvious choice for king, but his downfall was a fiery ego that often dictated dark moves. Belittling the prophets with choices that served his own political advances in opposition to God's word, Saul moved further away from God's calling on his life.

For years, the Prophet Samuel had observed Saul's growing recklessness with concern, watching with sorrow as the kingdom suffered from his hasty, thoughtless choices. One night, Saul crossed a line with disastrous consequences and God spoke to Samuel,

I regret that I have made Saul king, because he has turned away from Me and has not carried out my instructions.

Samuel wrestled with these words, tossing all night and perhaps begging God to change His mind. At dawn, he confronted the king with God's perspective. Angry, defensive, and insecure, Saul would hear none of the prophet's words. Moved with grief and disappointment as he recalled this man's potential, Samuel turned to leave the king he had anointed with his own hands, knowing he had done all he could do. Soon, the voice of God spoke again.

How long will you mourn for Saul? God asked. *Fill your horn with oil and go-- I have seen a king among Jesse's sons.*

Samuel resisted the idea. Perhaps he prayed, *I placed all my hopes in King Saul, and You want me to anoint another king?! Can't You just fix this one? Why should I risk hoping in another vision when this one ended so poorly?* Terrified, he wondered if Saul would hear of the errand and attempt to murder him.

"Lord," he wrestled, "This is not the politically-correct time to select a new king!"

God knew of his thoughts and responded,

I will show you what to do, and you will anoint unto Me the man who I tell you to.

In spite of his misgivings, Samuel filled his horn with oil, journeyed to the farm community of Bethlehem, and invited Jesse to a feast. Seven sons accompanied their father and stood to greet the prophet who eyed each of them closely, searching for the signs of royalty. A strong warrior in his prime, Eliab looked like a king to Samuel and he thought, Surely this is the Lord's man!

Reading his thoughts, the Lord quickly responded,

Don't look at his outward appearance or height: I have refused him. The Lord doesn't see as man sees. People look at the outward appearance, but I look at the heart.

Wisely, Samuel moved past the young man and scanned the rest of the family. However, the Lord was silent, identifying none of them as the new king. All eyes were fixed on the prophet, waiting for him to speak. As the moments ticked by with no direction from the Lord, Samuel shook his head, refusing to anoint any of the strapping young men in front of him until he received clarity.

The Lord would not have brought me here for no reason, he pondered. *Perhaps I am missing something.* Turning to their father, he asked curiously,

"Are all your children here?" The grey-bearded man shifted slightly and confessed,

"There is one more: the youngest. He's watching the sheep."

Immediately Samuel realized that God's hand was at work.

"Call him!" he said, a ring of triumph in his voice. "We will not eat until he arrives."

Still a teenager, sun burnt and freckled, the young shepherd boy was brought to the prophet. Innocent yet strong, with a harp over his shoulder and a lilt in his step, David approached with wonder. Weeks in the field had made his heart strong in praise to God, and he had learned the basic skills of leadership by protecting the helpless sheep.

Arise and anoint him, the Lord whispered to Samuel. *This is he.*

As his brothers watched in complete skepticism and disbelief, Samuel poured sacred oil over God's choice for a king: David, a shepherd boy, the man after God's own heart. It was a brand new dynasty born out of frustration, regret, and curious questions that revealed the purpose of God.

"Unless God has raised you up for this very thing,
you will be worn out by the opposition of men and devils.
But if God be for you, who can be against you?
Are all of them together stronger than God?

O be not weary of well doing!"
- John Wesley

When God brings a new vision into our lives, it sometimes comes during a season of frustration and disillusionment. We may wonder why He hasn't answered our prayers or why He isn't "fixing" things with easy solutions. Other times you may think, I have received prophetic words and it doesn't look like they are coming to pass! You may be in the position of Samuel who followed God's orders and still found himself facing the "no" of God even while being obedient to His will.

In studying the character of Samuel, I see two decisions that enabled him to see the new plan of God unfold: first, he stayed obedient and didn't quit, and secondly, he asked a good, probing question. Here's a few things we can learn from this story.

STAYING OBEDIENT

It would have been easy for Samuel to give up on his calling after seeing Saul, the man who he had anointed as king, make such a mess of things. He could have blamed himself, doubted God, or given up on his assignment. Instead, he got up and followed God's orders to do the very same thing again and anoint David as king. Why? Simply because he chose to obey.

Men and women who have accomplished amazing things for God always have one thing in common: a passion for obedience. You cannot make a dream come true simply because you "want" it enough – you have to choose to love God more than anything, and choose to put obedience to Him before everything else. Sometimes, He uses little things to test our obedience, and we have to be willing to accept His "no" before moving forward.

One time, I was building a ministry team and praying over who to invite. I really felt like my friend Jill would be a great addition to the team, but as I chatted with her on the phone, the Holy Spirit said, *She's not supposed to be involved that way.* I groaned inside and wondered how I was going to un-invite her, so I asked if we could pray together. Sure enough, I sensed in my heart that it was simply not the right connection. Slowly, I told her,

"I feel kind of weird, but the Lord is showing me that this isn't the right fit. Can we connect in another way concerning this vision?"

"Oh, that's a relief," she said, "because I felt the same thing and was going to decline your invitation!"

We laughed and were both so relieved that we could be honest with each other. Later, God brought just the right people for my team, and Jill and I are still great friends. Looking back, I can see why He was saying "no" to the first idea, but I simply couldn't have known what was coming at the time.

If Samuel had been more focused on the vision of anointing a new king rather than being obedient to God, he would have chosen the wrong man! Wouldn't that have been a mess?! As much as we can get excited about a vision coming to pass, it's important not to allow that dream to become an idol. To keep things in proper perspective, we must value obedience to God more than the vision. Believe me, I haven't always made the right choices in this area! There have been so many times I've gotten ahead of God and need to go back and repent for not listening to His gentle voice of guidance, but when I listen and obey, I'm always glad I did!

ASK GOOD QUESTIONS

When standing before Jesse's sons and realizing that the right one wasn't there, Samuel found himself in a difficult moment. He could have said,

"Oh well, God obviously doesn't know what He's talking about. Let Him find His own king!"

Instead, he turned the question on Jesse and put pressure on the situation to reveal God's plan by saying,

"Are these all your sons?"

When Jesse responded that there was one more, Samuel was so confident God had a plan that he refused to eat until the young shepherd arrived. David was hidden to everyone else, but the prophet moved foreseeable facts to discover that there was more than met the eye. As a result, God's plan was revealed, and Israel's new king was anointed!

When we come to a difficult place in our vision where it looks like a dead end, we have two choices: to give up, or ask questions. It may be that hidden treasure is waiting for someone to find it, and if God has brought you this far, He will give you the wisdom to seek it out.

"My mother made me a scientist without ever intending to.
Every other Jewish mother in Brooklyn
would ask her child after school,
"So? Did you learn anything today?"

But not my mother.

"Izzy," she would say, "did you ask a good question today?"
That difference—asking good questions
made me become a scientist."

– Nobel winner Isidor Isaac Rabi

FINDING THE TREASURE

Often God disguises His plan, possibly to test those who are destined to inherit it to see how much they truly want it. People frequently ask me how to handle the frustration they feel over promises or prophetic words they don't see coming to pass. How do we handle dreams that don't seem to be going anywhere? One secret to finding God's hidden treasure is to become very curious and ask Him questions. The scriptures encourage us to dig deep into the heart of God in our quest for answers.

It is the glory of God to conceal a matter,
But the glory of kings is to search out a matter.
Proverbs 25:2

The word "conceal" in Hebrew means: **to hide by covering.** The words "to search out" means, *to penetrate, examine intimately, search, seek out.* When God gives you a vision, it's often like a treasure hunt: He doesn't hand over the final prize immediately, rather, He wants you to find clues along the way and enjoy His companionship as you do it with Him. Recognize that a vision from God is an invitation to partner with Him. He invites you to think, reason, and ask Him curious questions. If you keep this childlike heart, you'll be enthralled by His wisdom, wit, and deep love for you throughout the process!

When I was a kid, my parents made treasure hunts for each of their children's birthdays. Sometimes we'd roll our eyes in frustration because we wanted an "easy gift," but soon we'd get excited as the hunt progressed. Handwritten clues led to more clues and sometimes a treasure map as we followed the trail to the goody bags of treasure. Our parents watched with glee as we learned to reason, ponder, and find our way through the puzzles, knowing that they'd crafted the whole thing for us to enjoy. I remember discovering one treasure hidden under the dining room table where I had just eaten my dinner without any idea of what was waiting for me underneath it!

Dreams from God are often like this: they require some clues and digging to find the path that leads to the treasure. Like a father who gleefully conceals a treasure for us to find, He knows that we will learn from the process and become wiser if we don't give up. I can't say that I've mastered this yet, but I will say it's been so much fun to find God in the journey.

FINDING TREASURE

When I started my first TV show, it began with a "treasure hunt" step of obedience. I had filmed a little DVD project with a hand-held camcorder, and I can't say it was very good, but I'd done my best. By no means was I a producer, and I certainly had no interest in being behind a camera, since my real ambition was to speak and sing on stage. One day, a visiting prophet came to my town and I deeply respected his ability to hear from the Lord. Every word he had spoken over me had been correct in the past, and I didn't take him lightly. That day he prayed over me and said,

"I really see you moving more and more in the creative arts for the Kingdom of God."

He didn't say it, but suddenly I knew that God was calling me to start a local TV show. I was horrified – it had taken me an entire year of struggle to create my little DVD, and I could only guess how much effort it would require to film and produce a TV show. Besides, I wanted to sing, not use the creative arts or produce television shows! I cried for two weeks, but in the end, I told God I would follow His call. So, I purchased the largest, shoulder-mounted video camera I could find (thinking it would give me more clout – it probably did!), bought some professional video editing software, and called all my artist friends and asked them on my variety show.

Little did I know, there was great treasure hidden in following this command from the Lord! People began to call me in tears, telling me they'd given up on their artistic gift, but the fact that I had invited them on my show had given them hope that God could still use them! I began to interview national music artists who were on tour in our small town and asked questions of some of the most talented men and women in Christian music. Because of these new opportunities and relationships, I ended up traveling the world, recording music videos, producing an EP with an award winning artist, and after a few years of hard work, my little show ended up airing on the largest Christian TV network in the world: all because I said yes to God and discovered the hidden gem in the journey.

I look back at that struggle and recall that the emotions were real: the frustration of being led a different direction that I'd hoped, the disillusionment of having to let a dream go, and the dread of going through the learning curve of discovering how to run new equipment. The wrestling was real, but the reward was great. Today, nearly all the doors open to me on various platforms are because I said yes to God's call at a critical moment and found the treasure hidden inside the journey of obedience.

ART FROM THE STRUGGLE

Of all the art in the Bible, it's fascinating to note how many songs and poems were born from prayers of struggle and seeking. One of the temple singers named Habakkuk was so brash in his wrestling with God that the

Jewish people actually took offense and rewrote his text to sound less shocking! According to Jewish tradition, the prophet-was a Levite psalmist who led the temple singing and at some point entered into a wrestling match with God. A disillusioned visionary, he couldn't understand why God was turning a deaf ear to the wickedness of the earth and allowing people to get away with evil. After pouring out his complaint to God, he makes a statement that I love! Basically, he says,

"Ok, Lord, I'm going to set up camp and wait for You to respond. I know I'm probably seeing this all wrong and that You will correct me, so I'll wait on Your answer."

It may sound arrogant, but God answered! His words took the prophet's breath away with wonder, proving that He wasn't oblivious to the turmoil on earth and He did have a plan. The last chapter of Habakkuk's book is a psalm pouring out praise and confidence to God, including the well-known words,

The LORD GOD is my strength and He will make my feet like hinds' feet, and He will make me to walk upon my high places.

Like Habakkuk, some of our best vision and art come from a place of wrestling with God where we simply need Him to show up and speak to our heart. The thing I love best about this story is that Habakkuk's name means "embrace," as though the entire chronicle is less like a wrestling match and more like a dance from heaven's perspective. As we ask questions, seek out answers, and delight in hearing from our Father, we can grow in this holy dance and discover beautiful wisdom that fuels our creative journey.

GOD IN THE WAY

So if you've felt discouraged or disillusioned by unfulfilled promises or dreams from the past, be tenacious. This journey is not just about seeing your dreams happen, but about going after God's heart and seeking His plan to move forward, knowing that He believes in your ability to walk with Him. I used to think that if God loved my dreams, He would give me huge opportunities and fling doors open to launch me into the public arena! Now I'm intensely grateful that He loves me more than He wants to use me, and He loves journeying with me through each door that opens. In fact, He goes ahead of me to prepare the way for each step of the process! One of my favorite verses about this is Psalm 21:1-3 in the King James Version:

The king shall joy in thy strength, O Lord;
and in thy salvation how greatly shall he rejoice!
Thou hast given him his heart's desire, and hast not withholden
the request of his lips. Selah.
*For thou **preventest** him with the blessings of goodness: thou*
settest a crown of pure gold on his head.

The old English word, "preventest" attempts to define the Hebrew word which means, *to project oneself, precede, anticipate, hasten, meet.* The best way I can identify with this is to think of my dad who is disabled and needs some extra care. I was his caregiver for many years and was constantly on the lookout for what he might need. Always a "step ahead," I would anticipate the things he required before he even had the chance to think about it, and this was simply a way I could show my care for him. When I read this verse, I realized that God cares for us the same way! He is constantly a step ahead of us, putting Himself in the way so that He can provide for the next step of our journey.

Repeatedly, I've seen this happen in the creative process! If I'll just do the "next right thing" in the process, He has the next step ready for me to step into. He loves us so much that He literally places Himself in our path to anticipate the next step. If we'll follow Him one step at a time, we'll discover that He's always ahead of us and right on time!

Launch the Vision

ASK YOURSELF:

1) Have you ever felt disappointed when your vision didn't happen in the past?

_____

_____

_____

_____

_____

_____

_____

2) What does it mean to "wrestle" with God?

_____

_____

_____

_____

_____

_____

_____

3) What are some of the questions that you wrestle with?

_____

_____

_____

_____

_____

_____

_____

4) Are there places of struggle that have added to your artistic journey?

_____

_____

_____

_____

_____

_____

_____

5) Like Samuel, have you ever heard God say "no" when you were stepping out to obey Him?

_____

_____

_____

_____

_____

_____

6) If so, how did you respond?

_____

_____

_____

_____

_____

_____

7) What are some "curious" questions you can ask God?

_____

_____

_____

_____

_____

_____

_____

8) Listen and write down anything He may speak.

_____

_____

_____

_____

_____

_____

9) What does it mean to see the creative journey as a dance with God?

_____

_____

_____

_____

_____

_____

10) How are you embracing that journey?

_____

_____

_____

_____

_____

_____

_____

PART II

AIM:
CREATING A STRATEGY
FOR YOUR VISION

"A vision without a strategy remains an illusion."
- Lee Bolman

"Hope is not a strategy."
-Vince Lombardi

LAUNCH THE VISION

CHAPTER FOUR
SEEDS

Dreams are the seeds of change.
Nothing ever grows without a seed,
and nothing ever changes without a dream.
– Debby Boone

After 17 years of being a full-time creative, I've created an organic strategy that seems to apply to every type of vision that helps launch a project from the "idea phase" to actually watching God touch lives with that vision. Whether I'm birthing a book, music CD, TV show, or planning an event, my process is the same, and I believe it will apply to you too!

FORMULA VERSES STRATEGY

First, let me make this point: babies need formula, but kings use strategies. A healthy baby needs his food processed into an easily digested milk (or, formula) so he can eat it without too much difficulty. Many people look for a "formula" to pursue their dreams that's easy, has three steps, and gets them quickly to their goals. However, I'm not here to give you a magic formula for your dreams: instead, I want to give you a Kingdom strategy that you can adapt and apply to your own vision. A strategy, in contrast to a formula, is not intended to be easy. It will stretch you, make you think, cause you to seek the face of God, and help you develop a plan of action that can launch your vision to the next level. Strategy is what kings use to build a kingdom, win a battle, and rule nations.

My particular strategy often comes into play during the most unusual of circumstances, and none more so that when He sent me on a mission to travel the world and create a TV show. It started like this...

Living in Nashville, TN area as a working artist was a dream come true, and I loved this city where so many artists were pursuing their dreams with passion. However, I could feel my heart getting restless and I wondered if God was up to something new, so I wasn't completely surprised to hear that my housing situation was not going to be available for much longer.

For the first week of each year, the local House of Prayer opened their doors 24/7 to anyone who wanted to pray, and I decided to take that opportunity to bombard heaven in search of some clarity for my next season. The first day,

I sat on the floor and simply cried out to God for direction. Worshiping, journaling, and pouring out my heart in prayer, I just asked for wisdom and waited.

Day two came, and in the quiet intimacy of the prayer room, I heard the voice of the Father speak.

Remember that idea you had to create a TV show for women with makeovers from around the world? That's not just your idea, that's My idea too.

That was all I needed. I picked myself up off the carpet and began to brainstorm a trip that would eventually take me around the world with my camera. Starting with the people I knew, I called the director of a girls' home in Arizona and an author in California. Both agreed to help with the vision of creating a TV show for today's women called, *Radical Makeovers.* Little did we know that I would interview 50 women in 7 countries, create 18 episodes of the show that would be translated into various languages, and that several years later a major publisher would contract me to create a book chronicling their stories and the amazing film journey.

Early the next morning, I received a message from the prayer room director who also managed a resale store with a warehouse full of donations.

"Come by the shop," she said, "I want to donate to your ministry." (She had no idea what God had spoken to me on the floor of her prayer room the day before!) Walking through the mounds of donated items, she encouraged me to select anything I could use. I emerged with both arms full of ball gowns which I traveled around the world with.

In awe, I realized that when God meets you in the secret place and puts His "go" on your vision, He shows up in miraculous ways.

Over and over I've seen this first strategic step bring so much fruit: **if you want God's blessing, take your vision into the secret place.**

> *"What wings are to a bird, and sails to a ship,*
> *so is prayer to the soul."*
> – Corrie Ten Boom

PLANT THE SEED

Your vision is like a seed: the entire DNA of your idea is wrapped up in your vision, just like a seed carries the potential to birth a tree. For that seed to germinate and put down roots, it has to be buried in the ground. For your vision to begin to come alive, it must be buried in the secret place of prayer. God repeatedly does this with me: He calls me into the quiet, hidden place where I can dream with Him, lay the vision before Him, and pray over the specifics with Him. During that time, I receive all the "DNA" needed for the vision.

The secret place is also where we receive the authority to actually carry out the vision. When I heard God say, *This isn't just your idea, it's My idea too,* I knew He would provide everything needed, because that's what He does for the visions He births. I have a lot of great ideas, but not all of them are anointed by God! In fact, I dare not move on some of them until I hear clearly from the Lord that He is giving me the signal to go ahead! This is very crucial if we're going to create with Him: we have all been given gifts and ideas, but our authority to create with His Presence comes in the secret place of prayer.

I once wrote a song for my Parables CD that emphasized both the human frustration and the beauty of being buried underground like a seed. Imagining the idea of a little seed admiring the tall trees and asking the gardener to carry him up to the sky to be like them, I wondered what a seed would "feel like" if the gardener told him that the way to become a tall tree was to first be buried underground. Nevertheless, the Father's love is revealed at each stage of the process: both underground and as the tree towers into the sky.

Once there was a seed Who kept looking at a tree
Every day his longing gaze Wished that he could be
The gardener, he said, "Son, this is what the Father meant
Even a little mustard seed Will grow into a tree

"And every little dream He's written in your heart
Is just a little seed Dreaming of the trees above
This is His love"

And so that little seed said, "Gardener, please carry me
So I can climb up in the sky Like a giant tree"
The gardener, he smiled, "And he said, "Son, you'll have to wait
a while
'Cause if you want to live up high First, you must die"

Cause every little seed Gets buried in the ground
For roots to grow down deep The Father meets you
underground
And this too is love

So that little seed Trembled as they buried
All his hopes and dreams Out of sight underground
And his shell began to crack 'Though he tried to keep the walls
intact
But they were like a worn out skin Next to the life inside of him
And though nobody could see Him turn into a tree
The Father held him close and said, This is My love

And he began to grow As he put roots into that fertile soil
Of the Father's love And poked his head into the sun
And now that little tree Tells everyone he sees
Not to be afraid Of dreams the Father made for them
'Cause this is His love

Each step of this process is a way to experience the Father's love and intimate connection to our lives, even the "burying!" If we truly want to partner with God and have His anointing on our vision, we can find it in the secret place of prayer where we dream with Him.

FATHER IN THE SECRET PLACE
When I was about five-years-old, this idea of the secret place became ingrained in my heart in a funny little way.

My little brother and I had this rambunctious tendency to avoid bedtime by slipping into each other's rooms and playing instead of sleeping. My dad decided to enforce bedtime, so he set up a wooden chair in the hallway between our rooms and made himself comfortable to keep watch until we fell asleep. With the "fear of dad" in our hearts, we kept our little bodies buried beneath the covers and quickly fell asleep. Funny enough, I recall that my father always brought his Bible, highlight pens, and a notebook during those nighttime vigils, and I knew he was praying for us too. It was part of his "secret place" time with the Lord.

One day, at the age of five, I announced that I was going to pray and hear from God. My mother, busy in the kitchen, simply smiled sweetly at my declaration, so I marched upstairs and planted myself in the place where I figured God would hear me the best: dad's chair in the hallway. The minutes ticked by as I waited for a revelation. I can't recall whether I really heard the voice of God, but when I tromped downstairs, I told my mother, "I think God wants me to paint!" and pulled out my little set of toy water colors for the afternoon.

I laugh at this story now, but it has become a hallmark moment of my childhood because I believe God was wooing me into the Father's love and His creative pattern even then. It is still in the secret place of the Father's love that I can hear His voice prompt me to create beauty – whether holding my kiddie water colors at the kitchen table or a using film camera across the globe.

How do we connect with the Father in the secret place? Far from being passive in His Presence, there are some very strategic things we can do. I've discovered there's some powerful tools that we can use for the "secret place" time that really help us lay the foundation for the vision.

WRITE THE VISION

One of the most powerful things we can do is to move the vision out of our head and onto paper. When we get quiet enough to really write down what we see, suddenly we can start creating something that's bigger than just the thoughts that fly around in our minds. Putting pen to page is crucial, just as an architect creates a blueprint before building a structure. On paper, we can flesh out a vision before taking steps to move which saves time later.

Write the vision and make it plain on tablets,
that he may run who reads it.
Habakkuk 2:2

The word "plain" in Hebrew means: *to dig, explain, and declare.* Before we run with a vision, it helps to dig a bit deeper, take time for further explanation, and begin to write specifics so it's clear to ourselves and others. A mistake many dreamers make is that we want people to "run with" our vision before we have spent time crafting the idea and "making it plain" on paper beforehand. People are more likely to help you if you've spent time figuring out what your vision looks like and what you need to birth it.

Believe me, this doesn't always come naturally for a visionary! Early in my creative journey, I remember being in a small group and the leader asked us to go around the room and each describe the vision we carried. When my turn came around, I froze. Feeling like a deer in the headlights, I couldn't understand how I could be so full of passion and still feel so unable to articulate what God had called me to do! It took several months of processing with mentors until I was able to clearly verbalize my heart and then make goals based on that vision. Once I could articulate my heart, doors opened so much easier and I was able to steer my creative energy in focused ways that could bring forth real fruit.

As you write your vision, take some time to think about what stirs your heart the most. It's those places of passion that will keep the vision fresh and exciting to you, and they will also be what appeal to others, because people are drawn to passion. What is the cause you are fighting for? Where is the need your vision will fill? What message are you carrying that the world needs to hear?

Here's some ideas of what to write:

1) Write a vision statement

I must confess, it took me a long time to figure out how important this step is! Now I wonder how I lived without it, because it makes life SO much easier. A vision statement is a description of your core values in just a few sentences. It can be hard for a visionary to narrow down a vision to a brief phrase or two, but simplicity is one of the keys to making your vision happen. For instance, when I wanted to start a ministry, I chose three core goals:

The Potter's House Vision
To Cultivate:
-A space for God's Presence
-A holy tribe of disciples who love well
-Creative arts with passion and excellence

That's it! I can write pages and pages of vision around these core values, and having a center point to base every other activity around is a marvelous help in staying focused. Creating a vision statement also helps narrow your focus and communicate it well so that other people can get excited about it too.

2) Craft your Goals

This step doesn't have to be set in stone, but it's a great way to start being practical with your dream. Sometimes I ask people about their goals and they respond,

"I just want to touch the entire world with my art and go as far as God will take me."

Right then, I get the idea that they haven't been very practical with their goals because they really don't have a starting point. God can launch any one of us into global ministry, but let's face it: most of the time, He asks us to start in our community or with a specific goal. Typically the people He launches into worldwide ministry are those who have been working hard already. He promotes those who are faithful, so what are you being faithful with? What's a good goal that you can see yourself achieving? Not something so high that's impossible, but something that will stretch your faith and be a good launching place to go higher? Who will your vision impact? What is your audience? Who will fall in love with your idea? Dream with God about your goals and set some ideas on paper, realizing that He can expand and tweak them along the way. Give yourself some good goals to start with!

3) Dream Big

Often I ask myself, *If I could do anything with this vision, what would it look like?* I recall one time when I was vision-casting for a film about spiritual warfare. I had some great actors and sword fighters, but the landscape in TX wasn't a very epic backdrop. During a phone call to a friend I mentioned,

"If I could do anything, I'd pack up my actors and go film in Alaska. I have friends up there and the scenery is stunning."

"Well," my friend responded, "why don't you?"

Stunned, I realized I hadn't even considered the possibility because I thought it was "too big." After calling a few friends in Alaska and crunching some numbers, I texted my actors.

"How would you like to film in Alaska for a week?"

Six of us packed our bags, took extra luggage with props

and costumes, and prayed for good weather as we filmed for a week in Alaska. That film has gone around the world and touched thousands of lives because we decided to dream big.

When writing your vision, don't be afraid to think about a big dream when creating the project. Refrain from writing down what you want to happen as the end result, like, *I want God to use me in mighty ways,* and focus on what you see happening in the creative process. Write down your vision with as much detail as you can think of, and begin to ask God for even bigger ideas than you can come up with on your own!

THE SIGNIFICANCE OF WRITING THE VISION

I truly believe something beautiful happens when we write our vision on paper, especially if we spend time praying over that vision. I learned this in a curious way when I first started dreaming with God...

When I was 17, I had a dream that felt enormous, but I couldn't help hoping and praying it would come true. I'd always dreamed of singing my little original songs on stage, and I desperately wanted to share my music with my favorite recording artist that I heard on the radio. I happened to meet him one day at a backstage event, and out of the goodness of his heart, he took a moment to pray for me. After that, I really wanted to reconnect with this man who played the piano and wrote pop songs, because I somehow felt like he could tell me if my music was any good. After about two years of desperately praying and hoping that I could somehow share my songs with him, a mentor gave me a piece of advice.

"Sometimes," she said in a matter-of-fact tone, "you just need to write your request and lay it before the Lord. If it's meant to be, He'll make a way. If not, then move on with your life."

So, I did: I wrote my request, laid it on my bedroom floor, and prayed. Nothing happened, so I buried the dream for about three years, moved across the state, and stopped writing songs. During that time, I had some profound encounters with God and started to pick up music again and express myself in worship to God. One day, I happened to be driving through the town I used to live in and noticed that my favorite pop star was doing a benefit concert and dinner in a local church. I decided to go, but I only had enough money for a concert ticket and not the meal beforehand. A funny thing happened that night when I arrived to the church early and asked to meet with the pastor.

"Do you happen to have a little corner where I could pray?" I asked politely. "I'm coming to the concert, but I don't have a ticket to the dinner."

To my surprise, the pop singer appeared and to my astonishment he remembered me from several years ago!

"Would you be my guest for the dinner?" he asked, and then he proceeded to walk to the ticket table and purchase me a ticket with cash from his own wallet.

Then he asked me to help him with the sound check, so I sat at the shiny grand piano in a daze, playing one of my little songs just like I had dreamed of doing years before. During dinner, I asked him every single question I'd ever wondered about the music industry, and he graciously responded. God had seen the prayer I had written down and laid before Him several years earlier, and just when He was about to call me into full time ministry and knew I would need some extra courage, He made my dream come true!

My point is this: God hears our prayers, but there is something special about writing down our dreams and vision. Time and time again, I've seen God's plans unfold in ways that leave me startled with a sense of wonder and awe, and many of these are dreams that I've written down and laid before Him. It's a beautiful thing.

BOLDNESS IN PRAYER

The Scriptures tell us that God publicly honors what happens in the secret place of prayer.

> *But you, when you pray, go into your room,*
> *and when you have shut your door,*
> *pray to your Father who is in the secret place;*
> *and your Father who sees in secret will reward you openly.*
> Matthew 6:6

After I write my vision, I often lay it on the floor, get on my knees, and begin to pray. That moment is a sacred space and I believe it sets the tone for the rest of my project, as I dedicate it to God and ask for His help in making it happen. We know that He hears and honors those who seek His face in secret, so make good use of this time!

ASK YOURSELF:

1) Does the idea of being "buried under ground" pique your interest or discourage you?

_____

_____

_____

_____

_____

_____

_____

2) How do you feel about inviting God into the "dreaming stage" of your vision?

_____

_____

_____

_____

_____

_____

3) Have you ever taken time to write your vision and make it plain?

_____

_____

_____

_____

4) Have you written clearly in ways that it would make sense to others?

_____

_____

_____

_____

_____

_____

5) What is your vision statement?

_____

_____

_____

_____

_____

6) What are your goals?

_____

_____

_____

_____

_____

_____

7) What are several emotions that define how your vision makes you feel?

_____

_____

_____

_____

_____

_____

_____

8) How does your vision impact others?

_____

_____

_____

_____

_____

_____

9) Does your vision reflect the heart of God? How?

_____

_____

_____

_____

_____

_____

10) Once you've written your vision, have you laid it before God in prayer?

_____

_____

_____

_____

_____

_____

_____

Launch the Vision

CHAPTER FIVE
STRATEGY

It may be hard for an egg to turn into a bird:
it would be a jolly sight harder for it to learn to fly while
remaining an egg.
We are like eggs at present.
And you cannot go on indefinitely being just
an ordinary, decent egg.
We must be hatched or go bad.
– C. S. Lewis

At the age of 15, I fell in love... with a brown, Arabian horse named Saruk. He was the most beautiful gelding I had ever seen, so gentle with intelligent eyes, and my neighbors who had raised him from a foal decided that I could buy him and take him home. There was just one problem: Saruk was six-years-old and had never been trained. He wasn't as gentle as he looked!

I had the romantic idea that we would simply bond (like all the movies I loved about horses and girls) and come to a mutual understanding that I was his owner and he would follow my lead. I vowed never to put a bridle in his mouth and decided I would use leg cues to communicate while riding. This idea worked rather well and I even rode him a bit, but there was a hidden problem: Saruk was terrified of... well, almost anything. At the drop of a hat he would panic and bolt, and I would lose all control. I was thrown into a barbed wire fence, dragged on the ground by a stirrup, and sprained my ankle and had to spend a week on crutches, all because of this fearful habit. So we never really galloped together as I had imagined. We just walked a lot, Saruk got fat in the pasture, and I lived with a nagging sense of failure as a horsewoman.

One day he bucked a friend of mine off and I got mad. So mad, that I called a trainer and sent him to a stable for a month. This man with a cowboy hat and spurs on his boots had very little mercy. He put a bit in Saruk's mouth, shoes on his feet, and refused to spoil him. I was terrified -- he was ruining my baby! I was also relieved that someone else was doing what I didn't have the courage to do: be a leader for my horse.

At the end of the month, Saruk was a new horse. Still rough around the edges, I stabled him at a friend's house who had an 800-acre ranch, and we rode for hours so I could work through his rough spots. I got some training and figured out how to be a better communicator and not let him run over me, and I even learned how to discipline him in practical ways that never harmed him. (I used a bit and bridle, too.) After a few months, my dream came true: I could just think a command and barely shift in the saddle, and Saruk obeyed. His over-sensitivity was now tuned to hearing my voice, and he could easily move at just the slightest of commands. We had so much fun racing over fields and galloping through open glens together!

Over the years, I've had a lot of romantic ideas about art and ministry. Like my horse experience, I thought the vision would "just happen" since the idea had so much potential. One of the biggest mistakes I made was believing that God would snap His fingers and give me a "big break" to instantly propel me to greatness. Actually, His process is way more fun than that! Instead of giving a single "wow moment," He loves to answer our prayers in dozens of ways that really blow our minds along the journey to our goals. His goal is not just for us to "fall in love" with an idea, but learn to walk so closely with Him that we become one -- just as I did with my horse-- until we move together and go to beautiful places.

People often ask me, *How do you take a vision from what's in your head to a finished product?* In this chapter we'll talk about how to build a Biblical strategy and why this is important. There's a difference between faith and romance: one works, and the other is just nice ideas. I'm praying that as you read this, the parts that will apply to you will burn in your heart and you'll sense the Holy Spirit leading you. Just like my horse example, it will require some work and sharpening of ideas and skills. It might take more work than you think, but you'll be moving forward and taking leadership that will help your goals come to pass!

An example of what this looks like can be found in the Biblical account of Nehemiah, who was not only a visionary, but a great strategist.

PREPARING FOR KINGS

Nehemiah is a great example of a man who had a vision and brought it to pass. When he heard that his home city of Jerusalem had been burned and destroyed, he went into the secret place of prayer and began to cry out to God. Moved with a vision to rebuild the walls, he did more than pray-- he became a man of strategy.

The king of Babylon sensed that something was on Nehemiah's heart, and asked him to tell his vision. Boldly sharing his idea, Nehemiah's heart must have skipped a beat when the king responded,

"What is your request?"

Inwardly, Nehemiah whispered a quick prayer for wisdom.

"If it seems good to you, send me to Jerusalem." he said. "Write a letter of safe conduct that will secure safe passage through the territories and a letter to Asaph the keeper of the lumber to give me all the wood needed to rebuild."

Graciously, the king granted every request, and Nehemiah's vision started to become reality.

God has "kings" waiting to help you build, but you need more than vision: you need a strategy. When a person of influence asks you, "What do you need for your vision?" they're not going to listen to thirty minutes of a visionary expressing their hopes and dreams. Like the king, if you have a specific, itemized list of what you need to accomplish the work, there's a good chance they'll help you get there. If you're scattered with your thoughts, you probably will not hold their attention.

The most powerful tool you can offer yourself is to condense your vision into a strategy that is clear to the rest of the world! If you itemize the steps, there are so many "kings" who are ready to help bring it into reality. Notice how Nehemiah had done his homework: he mentions by name Asaph who was responsible for the lumber and requests the king to write several letters. He is precise, clear, and has made a way for others to be a part of his vision. Bottom line: kings will sow into your vision if it's inspiring, clear, and easy for them. Kings don't waste time on people who aren't ready.

BUILD YOUR STRATEGY

Think of your vision as an amazing chocolate cake. You can imagine how good it will smell and the rich, mouth-watering taste, so you open a recipe book and look at the ingredients involved in baking it. With a little strategy, skill, and instruction, you'll soon have a cake! Some of the ingredients you may already have and some you might have to purchase, but figuring that out will help you move forward toward experiencing that amazing goal.

Building your strategy for your vision is like baking a chocolate cake: you figure out what you have, what you need, and a way to fit it all together. As you think through the process and map out the path to your vision, start creating a list of what you'll need to make it happen. If it's a music CD, start thinking of the song list, musicians, a place to record, graphic design, and what kind of budget is required. For a film, start thinking of innovative locations, actors, and friends who could also be passionate to help with the project. When you itemize your vision, you'll have pieces you can take action on, and there are other areas you can start praying over for provision. You may already have people or items on hand that come into play, so you can already start checking things off your list. Sometimes I even pray crazy prayers that help me figure out where to start!

For one film production, I prayed, *God, if You want me to do this documentary, would You give me an interview with Heidi Baker?* She was booked to speak at a conference in my city, so I reached out to her management and requested an interview. Later I discovered that she had received five requests for interviews and mine was the only one she felt led to accept! (Lord, thank You for crazy favor!) That was my green light for the project, so I moved ahead with the film! Honestly, it was possibly the most difficult film I'd ever created, so I would need to remember that confirmation for encouragement later on.

By breaking down the vision into bite-sized pieces, we can start to trust God for those individual pieces, and He begins to answer prayers and open doors!

THINK LIKE A GUY

Sometimes we artists can become so absorbed in our vision that it's hard to organize our thoughts into a strategy. To help with this process, I tell my artists to "think like a guy!" Men tend to compartmentalize their thoughts. The idea that "men are like waffles" is true: they work within a certain box and focus on one thing, while women have a million connected thoughts all at once. Artists and visionaries sometimes need to step back from the big picture, compartmentalize their vision, and logically process the steps required to make it happen.

I've gotten pretty good at doing this, but sometimes I'll call a friend for help or ask some advice from a leader who can help me chart my creative explosion into a clear road map. Often, I still need help when it comes to writing. For instance, sometimes I have the vision for a book, but the idea of crafting chapters within that book can be totally daunting! If I have an editor or friend to process with, we can break down the vision and figure out how to communicate it well.

Whether you do this alone or with a friend (or several friends!), take some time to itemize the pieces that your vision will require in order to move forward, then start moving with what you have and pray over the rest. It's amazing how quickly things can come together when we do this!

BUILD YOUR COMMUNICATION

Jesus demonstrated the power of good communication: He could tell a parable in a few sentences that was so concise and rich with meaning that it needed no explanation. One of the things we often run into as visionaries is that our idea works in our head but leaves people scratching their heads and wondering what we really mean. Refining our communication is one of the most powerful things we can do as visionaries.

A mentor of mine once said,

"You can throw a steak at a dog and he will run from you, but if you serve it on a platter, he will eat out of your hand."

A good thing presented a confusing way won't accomplish it's purpose. However, if you refine your communication and presentation, you can fill a need that people have been craving. This is a great time to "test" your vision with some safe people in your life and see how well it connects with them. Do they get excited, or do their eyes glaze over when they hear it? Does the song you wrote, the book idea, or the film concept stir others like it does you? Of course, this means finding a group of safe people who will both applaud you and tell you the truth. My worship leader friend Dennis Jernigan says,

"My songs are like pearls. I don't want to cast my pearls

at people who will not appreciate them. Instead, I want to gather people around me who will help polish my pearls." Find a group of people who will encourage and affirm your ideas, as well as speak truth, and you'll begin to fine-tune your communication. Build your own "Inklings" group, where friendships akin to Tolkien and Lewis avail themselves as sounding boards as you share your vision.

BUILD YOUR SKILL

Keep in mind what skills you bring to the table that will help your vision. It's fun to bring skills that we wouldn't normally think of into the mix-- I know one woman who baked apple pies to raise funds for her vision! There may also be times when God will challenge us to learn some new skills to help launch our vision well.

When I first started speaking with my potter's wheel in churches, people began asking me for a DVD of my message, so I prayed for two years that God would send me a videographer. It didn't happen. Finally, I decided that maybe I should change my prayer, so I said,

"God, if You want me to film this myself, would You give me a camera?"

Two days later, a woman walked into the studio where I worked, and I happened to share my prayer with her.

"Oh," she said, "The Lord already told me to buy a video camera and donate it to the studio. Let's go to the store and buy one."

In shock, I hopped in her car and we drove to the electronics store to purchase a camera. With that little camera, I created a ministry video and even released it on the local TV channel. Apart from filming home videos as a kid, that was my first attempt at film making. There was a learning curve and lots of moments of frustration as I learned a technology that I really had no interest in, but film-making became a much bigger piece of my ministry than I had ever expected, and now my films are broadcasted all over the world.

Sometimes we are expecting a "king" like Nehemiah had to meet our needs, when the King of Kings actually wants to give us the skills required to make our goals happen. It may take a learning curve, but sometimes we are actually the very best "stewards" of our vision when we carry out pieces of it ourselves. Sometimes building new skills can be a great part of seeing God's plan unfold.

You can design and create, and build the most wonderful place in the world. But it takes people to make the dream a reality.
– Walt Disney

BUILD YOUR TEAM
Going back the story of Nehemiah, there came a time when he began to bring others into his vision, and he did this by telling them of God's favor with the king:

And I told them of the hand of my God which had been good upon me,

and also of the king's words that he had spoken to me.
So they said, "Let us rise up and build."
Then they set their hands to this good work.
Nehemiah 2:18

When the people saw God's favor on Nehemiah, they jumped on board. I believe Nehemiah had favor with the king because of his time spent in the secret place of prayer, and because his vision was a direct fulfillment of God's heart at that time. Interestingly, Nehemiah was not a prophet: he never received a supernatural command from God to rebuild the city. Instead, he was moved with passion for a cause, spent time in prayer, made a request to the king, and kept stepping out in faith. Eventually, he began to rally others to his cause, and they followed because they saw God's favor on his life.

If your vision is bigger than yourself, it will require a team of people to pull it off. It can be scary to invite people to partner with you, but it is also a lot of fun! Invite people you are close to as well as people who have a better or different skill set than you do. Each individual will add their touch to your creative project and it will often turn out much better than you expected.

For my film *Celtic Pilgrimage*, we used hundreds of actors and no one was paid a dime- except for one. (I needed one more extra for the shoot and told a friend I'd give him $50 to play a Druid!) It was absolutely amazing to see how many people jumped on board the vision for an afternoon or two. Others offered to host me in their spare bedroom when I filmed in Alaska or Ireland, and still others drove us hundreds of miles around various nations to help us capture the best footage. It was an incredible rallying of people around a cause we were all excited about: telling powerful, inspiring stories, and bringing glory to God. Plus, it was just plain fun!

For one shoot, I needed a 16' round table with 24 seats around it. A local carpenter donated his time and we created the table out of wood, Styrofoam, and layers of paint. I needed 24 kings and queens to sit around the table, representing leaders of the land, so I got the crazy idea to phone 24 pastors and Christian leaders in Southern California and ask them to dress up in costume and be part of the shoot. We filled the chairs and had a blast doing it! They even brought swords (it's amazing how many people own weapons!), and we laid them on the table along with candles. A drone pilot volunteered to fly his drone over the table for some aerial shots (the wind of his propellers put the candles out, but the shot looked cool!). You may need some big favor when building your team, but you'll have an amazing time doing it.

BUILD YOUR FAITH

When Jesus had a need, He often used what was in front of Him to meet it. Clay for a blind man's eyes... five loaves and two fish... a coin from a fish's mouth... a basin and towel. Using the simple, mundane things of life, He wove timeless stories that still touch hearts 2,000 years later. It didn't take a million dollars to spread the gospel, just a lot of love, the Holy Spirit, and some simple props to tell great stories.

So many times I've wished for a huge budget to create my films and projects, and sometimes God provides finances easily. Other times, He challenges me to look in front of me, and I'll see exactly what's needed, just waiting for me to pick it up. In the Western world, we're used to throwing money at projects in order to make them succeed, but true vision takes a lot more than finances! I've come to believe that we need anointed creativity even more than we need funds, and we need the faith to access the vision to see it. Knowing that God will move, we step out in faith and watch Him supply using really fun, creative means! Here's a few examples of how I've seen Him show up in this way.

Wool blanket: I was doing a bit of filming in Scotland and thought, *Wouldn't it be grand to film some reenactments of Celtic saints right here in the nation rather than staging it in the USA?* The difficulty was that I didn't have any costumes, and raw, woolen fabric is very difficult to find in the U.K.. After visiting several fabric shops, I started to pray in earnest, and happened to look in my wardrobe at the mission house where I was staying. Sitting on a shelf in my bedroom was a thick, grey woolen blanket the very color I needed for a medieval costume! Not only did the mission house donate their blanket for the costume, but they also offered the use of their sewing room. After a few hours, I had a woolen robe that was perfect for my film, and multiple actors wore that costume all over the hills of Scotland!

Thrifting Stylist: For my very first film, *Girl Perfect*, I needed a wardrobe to tell the story of a runway model. Having no concept of fashion or any clue about the world of the modeling industry, I called a friend of mine who had a knack for clothes. She studied designers, her house looked like a magazine, and she bought everything at thrift stores!

"Nancy," I asked, "would you be my wardrobe stylist for this film?"

No kidding- we styled that entire film for about $600, we found every piece of clothing from local, country thrift stores, and I learned how to spot Italian name brands I couldn't even pronounce. The shoots looked great, and I learned that having an eye for fashion is far more important than a thick wallet! Nancy was a great person to bring on board, because she could help me see what was right in front of my nose.

Extra Pirates: I remember one scene we were dramatizing for a film and I needed extras that afternoon. I was speaking at a local church and decided to ask the pastor if it was ok to give a call for extras that morning. It happened to be a call for Irish pirates, and sure enough, I had just enough men from the church volunteer to show up at the beach that afternoon for the scene. I even had to make a mad dash to the fabric store after church to throw together one last costume before the shoot! Funny enough, one of the pirate extras happened to have a background in theater and showed us some fun tricks that were helpful for the scene. He had visited the church for the first time that morning, and was blown away that someone had invited him into a film shoot! My team got to pray with him, and it was a perfect moment where my vision created an opportunity to encourage someone else along the way.

BUILD YOUR BUDGET

There are so many ways to finance your project, and sometimes it can be overwhelming to think about how much things cost. Jesus was very strategic about calling people to count the cost before jumping into vision that would call for a large investment.

For which of you, intending to build a tower,
does not sit down first and count the cost,
whether he has enough to finish it —

lest, after he has laid the foundation,
and is not able to finish,
all who see it begin to mock him, saying,
'This man began to build and was not able to finish'?
Luke 14:28-30

Counting the cost is a great part of building your vision. If you create an itemized breakdown of all your costs, it may be much more affordable than you think. Or, you may have to start praying and raising funds. Here's a few pointers:

- Kickstarter campaigns are a great way to allow your audience to cover the cost of a project. This way, you have an automatically built-in fan base to distribute to, and you keep all the rights to your creation.
- If you're writing a book, decide whether to publish or self-publish. Any publisher worth their salt will pay you to publish with them -- you shouldn't have to pay them. Make sure you read any fine print and "count the cost" with any platform that charges you.
- If you self-publish, make sure you consider the cost of a good editor, cover design, and layout within your budget.
- Itemize exactly what you need for your vision and figure out your budget. Then look over your list again and figure out if there's anyone you know who could help volunteer their time or even swap services to help you out. I often use volunteers and do most of the work myself which has enabled me to cut back on costs.
- Sometimes people will donate to your cause, so make sure you know what you need. If you're prepared, they are more likely to see your vision as a good investment.

Make sure that you explore lots of avenues for funding, and start with what you have!

BUILD YOUR PRAYER TEAM

Having prayer support is so crucial, especially as you move towards the release of your project. It could be as simple as a few close friends that you gather for coffee and ask to cover you in prayer as you launch. Often, we think that people may not be interested, but many people consider it a great honor to partner with you in prayer especially if they are moved by your vision. Ask them to pray for you during the process, and update them along the way. It's so powerful to know that people have your back, and that you also have a close circle of friends to be accountable to.

ANOINTED CREATIVITY TRUMPS MAJOR FUNDING

How many movies or music projects have we fallen in love with because they're raw, organic, and uncluttered by over-production? Compelled by passion, our souls are drawn like magnets to creativity in it's pure form. It takes daring courage to enter that place, but often it's the dreamers who simply use what they have who stumble upon marvelous beauty. Don't be afraid to pray and stretch your creativity in order to compensate for what you may not have at the moment! If we learn to use what's in front of us, we'll be able to team up with the Holy Spirit just like Jesus did in order to tell great stories and touch people's lives.

It's wonderful to watch people respond to anointed creativity. They recognize you don't have a Hollywood budget, but they also notice what is beautiful and real. One of my favorite comments came after a few friends watched one of my recent movie trailers. "Oh my," they exclaimed. "This isn't a low budget film!" I just laughed and thought, *This is probably the lowest budget film you've ever seen!* The truth was, they saw excellence, beauty, and an awesome story and that was compelling enough to draw them in. I didn't have a lot, but I asked the Lord to give me vision and then used what I had to make it happen. He rewards those who are faithful, and He always gives us more when we use what's in front of us!

ASK YOURSELF:

1) If you knew someone was ready to invest in your project, how would you prepare?

_____

_____

_____

_____

_____

_____

_____

2) What would happen if you started preparing now?

_____

_____

_____

_____

_____

_____

3) If you knew that God was about to promote you, what steps would you take to be ready?

_____

_____

_____

_____

_____

_____

4) What is in front of you that can be used to take the next step?

_____

_____

_____

_____

_____

_____

_____

5) What are some ways you can build your communication?

_____

_____

_____

_____

_____

_____

_____

6) What are some ways you can build your skill?

_____

_____

_____

_____

_____

_____

_____

7) What are some ways you can build your team?

_____

_____

_____

_____

_____

_____

_____

8) What are some ways you can build your faith?

_____

_____

_____

_____

_____

_____

_____

9) Are there things that have kept you back from moving forward with your strategy?

_____

_____

_____

_____

_____

_____

_____

10 What are some things you can do now?

_____

_____

_____

_____

_____

_____

_____

CHAPTER SIX
SHALOM

If I waited for perfection... I would never write a word.
– Margaret Atwood

Ever since I was a child, I dreamed I could fly. Sometimes it was easy to simply launch myself into the sky during my dreams, and other times I felt like a baby bird struggling to use her wings and barely getting off the ground. One dream interpreter has said that dreams of flying are often a sign that you're called to great faith. The more I study the creative process, the more I believe that it takes great faith to defy gravity and launch into what God calls us to do... it's a lot like flying.

Each creative process looks different, but the pull of "gravity" is real. Have you ever heard a little voice in your head whispering, *You'll never be good enough to get a recording contract... sign a book deal.. .or make a movie?* In a culture where media is constantly competing for our attention, it can be difficult to imagine we could produce anything "good enough" to be compelling. On top of that, sometimes the most difficult eye to please is our own. If you're a perfectionist, you may never finish a project because you think it's impossible to meet your own standards. We long to fly and launch our vision, but sometimes the most we can do is wistfully watch those above us who dare to spread their wings.

In this chapter, I'd like to tackle three English words (and concepts) that have limited many creatives and kept them "earth-bound." As you start moving forward with your vision, you'll be able to build momentum as you apply these tools and not get as bogged down by the process. As we unpack our understanding of these three words, we'll discover that our expectations may differ from God's, and it's our own mindset that clips our wings. Hold on tight: we're going deep!

PERFECTION
Lie: Perfection is the absence of flaws
Truth: Perfection is the place of wholeness, peace, and blessing

How many of us struggle with the tendency toward perfectionism? We become our own worst enemy because we're a tough critic! Artistic people are often harder on themselves than anyone else. Part of this thinking comes from the Western idea of the word *perfection*, and how that word differs from the Hebrew meaning. Not only do the two languages differ in their interpretation, but they could be called polar opposites. *Webster's Dictionary* defines the English word like this:

Perfect means:
a: being entirely without flaw or defect
b: satisfying all requirements
c: corresponding to an ideal standard or abstract concept

I don't know about you, but both I and my art are completely disqualified from that list! I can never rid myself of flaws, defects, or be able to satisfy all the requirements that people place on me. I don't even measure up to my own expectations sometimes! Compare this to the Hebrew definition: several words are used, but one word translated as *perfect* in our English language is the Hebrew word, *shalem*, which comes from the root word, *shalom*.

Shalom means:
To be safe (in mind, body, estate), to be completed, be friendly, make amends, peace
It carries an idea of "wholeness" and perfect peace because everything is fully satisfied, well, and whole. *Shalom* is the Hebrew greeting in Israel today, and they use it as Westerners would use the phrase, "Hello, have a good day!" It's a blessing of peace, prosperity, and blessing. We see it in this verse:

*Let your heart therefore be **perfect** with the LORD our God,*
to walk in his statutes, and keep his commandments,
as at this day.
1 Kings 8:61

According to this definition, a perfect heart is one that is whole, safe, and full of the Lord's peace.

Another word for "perfect" in the Hebrew is the word, *Tawmeem*, which means: *Entire, integrity, truth, without blemish, complete, full, undefiled, upright, whole.* Within this idea, we see that God is the one who brings this fullness into our lives: we don't have to figure it out or accomplish it alone. For example:

It is God that girdeth me with strength,
*and maketh my way **perfect.***
Psalm 18:32

While our English dictionary defines the word "perfect" by drawing attention to flaws and negative defects, the Hebrew idea is built on wholeness, safety, and being complete. It's an entirely different goal that suddenly sounds much more appealing and attainable! Of course without God, true wholeness and completion are impossible, but Colossians 2:10 tells us that we are already complete in Christ! Because of Christ's death and resurrection, we simply receive His grace to complete what we cannot on our own. There is no better way to fully live than from the place of knowing that God has already finished the work and we simply receive His free gift of grace and partner with Him to walk it out.

What if we applied this definition to our art? Are we trying to create in ways that are "entirely without flaw or defect," or are we aiming for "wholeness, fullness, and integrity" in our creative projects? Are we shooting for Shalom? If Webster's "perfection" is my goal, I'll never start! But with God's help, I believe that peace, wholeness, and completeness is possible for my creative projects. If you make this your goal with the Holy Spirit as your guide, you can get there too!

PERFECTION OR OBEDIENCE?

Earlier I mentioned how I started a TV show in my small town. If I'm honest, I'll admit that my program was pretty cheesy. I rigged up a green screen in my apartment, filmed in parks and on country roads, and talked all my artist friends into creating music videos. We did silly skits, interviews with local musicians, and everything was accomplished with one camera. It was the very best I could do, and even though it wasn't a high-dollar production, our community loved it. Lots of love and heart went into the making of that TV series!

One day, a famous songwriter came to town and spent time helping several local artists (including myself) record music albums. She mentored us and offered suggestions on how to improve our brand as artists.

"Quit the TV show," she told me. "Sorry, but it's so

unprofessional that it makes you look bad. People won't take you seriously as an artist if you continue."

I bit my lip and prayed. I knew my show wasn't that great, but our community loved it, and I had seen real fruit for God's Kingdom from the program. I prayed and asked God if He was calling me to end the show, but I didn't feel released from it, so I decided to ignore the producer's advice and keep filming the show for our local public access TV network.

Several years later, other local networks decided to pick up my show, and I started getting bigger interviews with well-known guests. Slowly, my technique and the show's quality improved, even though I was paying for everything out of my own pocket and it was still just me and my camera. My big dream was for the show to be broadcast on an international TV youth channel. One day I pitched this network my show, and the station manager called me.

"If you can take the quality of the show to the next level, we'd be interested in airing it." He gave me a list of ways to improve, and I immediately called my artist friends and shared the opportunity. They jumped on board and we worked hard to create some shows that were better than anything I had yet produced. The network picked it up, and soon my little program was being aired all over the world!

If I had allowed well-meaning advice to stop my show, I would have probably given up on filming all together. Instead, I hung in there and decided to keep going as long as there was Kingdom fruit resulting from it. If God wanted a girl with a camera, I was going to give Him my best! Today, my shows are on multiple worldwide networks, have been translated into various languages, and no one is more shocked than me!

My point is this: if you aim for Webster's definition of perfection, you may miss God's bigger plan. If you aim for obedience, you'll be free to do your best and simply trust that God will accept the level you're at and use it for His glory. My level of skill has changed over the years, and I hope it continues to get better. In ten years, I hope to have grown so much that I look back at my current work and roll my eyes! However, if you never start, you never grow, right? God loves our best efforts, and He is able to use them, so don't avoid obedience by being too hard on yourself.

I am careful not to confuse excellence with perfection.
Excellence I can reach for; perfection is God's business.
– Michael J. Fox

EXCELLENCE

Lie: God can use anything, so why aim for excellence?
Truth: Excellence will help you excel God's way!

We have all seen faith-based art that makes us cringe with its low quality. I'm not suggesting that we should release sloppy art and say, "Well, God can use anything!" Truthfully, if you're creating art you're passionate about, you should aim for it to be as excellent as possible at your stage of ability. However, let's remember that "excellent work" for a 1st grader is different than for a college student. Start with what you have, embrace humility, and aim for excellence as you grow.

Before I started ministry (while living in Deadwood), a visiting preacher from India spoke at a local church and I went to hear him. I was feeling desperately useless to the Kingdom of God, and couldn't see that I had any opportunity to bring forth any fruit for Christ. The man from India preached long and hard about how God offers us different things during our lifetime, saying,

"God will give you exactly what you are ready for. He is a good Father who will not give you more than you can handle. You don't give a baby a rifle, you give him a rattle. Later, when he is more mature, you entrust him with bigger things. If God gives you a rattle, shake it for all it's worth!"

From the wooden pew in that country church, I closed my eyes and thought,

What I have is very small, but I'll use it for God with everything I have! Maybe I only have a rattle, but I'll shake it with all my might!

This is what we aim for: excellence. It means giving God everything in order to make what you have become the best it can possibly be. If you truly want to aim high, you'll allow God to bring you out of mediocrity and into a place where your art shines with excellence. It really doesn't matter whether we have a rattle or a shotgun, the point is that we make the most of what we have and ask for His anointing, and God releases His blessing in proportion to what we offer in that season. It reminds me of the account of the widow's mite:

Now Jesus sat opposite the treasury
and saw how the people put money into the treasury.
And many who were rich put in much.
Then one poor widow came and threw in two mites...

So He called His disciples to Himself and said to them,

"Assuredly, I say to you that this poor widow
has put in more than all those who have given to the treasury;
for they all put in out of their abundance,
but she out of her poverty put in all that she had,
her whole livelihood."
Mark 12:41

This is a beautiful and scary passage of scripture, especially if we think of it in the context of our vision and creativity. It wasn't the gift with the most monetary value that held the greatest importance, but rather, Jesus placed worth on the small gift that was a great investment to the giver. The widow's heart was passionate about excellence, so she gave all she had. I believe that our creative process can be part of our worship. The beauty of God's Kingdom is that when we offer Him our best, regardless of how it looks or measures up to anyone else, He loves it and often uses it for His glory.

EXCELLENCE BRINGS FAVOR

People are impressed with excellence, and if they see that you are intentional about your work, they take you seriously. I can't tell you how many open doors I've had simply because people have seen that I take my work seriously. People instinctively can tell when you're intentional, professional, and have a heart to serve. Responsibility and graciousness go a long way when you're working with people who can open doors for you. Probably the greatest ingredients for success are a combination of humility mixed with confidence – if you are paying the price for releasing your vision well, it shows.

Do you see a man skilled in his work?
He will stand before kings;
He will not stand before obscure men.
Proverbs 22:29

EXTRAVAGANCE

Lie: "Extravagance" means "wasteful."
Truth: Use this concept to embrace your love for beauty and create a world of wonder.

How do we intentionally create with excellence? I discovered a secret key to unlocking this idea while at the Queen of England's gift shop. While visiting Buckingham palace, I slipped into the royal shop and was stunned by the beauty inside. Porcelain china dishes were glazed to the tiniest detail, jewels were intricately crafted, and extravagant attention was poured into the smallest of items. Amazed, I wandered from shelf to shelf, admiring the royal coat of arms hand-painted on a tea set, and ornate tins of biscuits all made with precision and care.

Extravagance is the mark of royalty, I mused, and began to ponder how good art carries great attention to detail. I wondered what it would be like to cultivate this "royal touch" in my art, investing special time into details that would make the audience pause to marvel at the beauty of God's Kingdom. **Extravagance is a key to creating a world of wonder.**

If you watch the "behind the scenes" features on movies, you'll understand this concept! Immense time and energy are invested into making costumes, not just to look good on camera, but to cause the actors to easily get in character. Props with intricate details may not even be seen on camera but help "set the mood" for the shoot. Hundreds of people create a set that makes the viewer believe that hobbit holes could really exist and wardrobes might actually have other worlds inside them. In a recent Cinderella movie, 2000 candles were lit by hand for the ballroom scene alone! Extravagant attention to detail is what makes us feel like the film is something we want to be a part of.

I started embedding this idea of "extravagant royalty" into my films. I invested extra time into hand-stitching my costumes and driving a few hours to get to a shoot location that would only be in the film for only a few minutes (or seconds). We spent long hours hot-gluing hundreds of jewels into crowns and sewing tailor-made costumes instead of renting them. One time I locked myself away in a spare room for a month to create 26 costumes for a scene. In Dublin, I scoured the city for a fabric shop that sold woolen tweed and unbleached wool so I could create authentic, Celtic costumes.

I wasn't aiming for perfection, but rather, extravagance! While sticking to a budget, **I intentionally invested in beauty.** I stayed thrifty and didn't waste money, but I strategically allowed myself to pull in beautiful details that were "eye candy" to the viewer and helped them connect with the story. To my delight, I discovered that God blessed this investment, especially when I partnered with His Holy Spirit in this process! Not only did He give me ideas of what to create, but I ran into the craziest bargains and finds in thrift stores and fabric shops that helped me obtain what I needed to tell beautiful stories.

If we look into scripture, we see that God uses extravagant beauty to speak to people. First, He creates a world full of it. How many flowers will never be seen but are stunning in their beauty? From the furthest star to the most fabulous sunset, we see how God lavishes His creation with extravagant, intentional beauty. Have you ever seen a peacock's feathers or a butterfly's wing? His attention to detail is proof of His love for beauty and the evidence of the riches of His Kingdom displayed for us to see every day. One mark of His royalty is the way He lavishes these riches on His creation.

Secondly, we see in Scripture how God partnered with an artist to create a work of art that was extravagant and costly, and it became a doorway to His Presence. When building the Tabernacle, a place filled with gold, prophetic symbols, and stunning craftsmanship, He singled out a man named Bezalel and said,

> *"See, I have called by name Bezalel the son of Uri,*
> *the son of Hur, of the tribe of Judah.*
>
> *I have filled him with the Spirit of God,*
> *in wisdom, and in understanding, and in knowledge,*
>
> *and in all manner of workmanship, to design artistic works,*
> *to work in gold, in silver, in bronze, in cutting jewels for*
> *setting,*
> *in carving wood, and to work in all manner of workmanship .*
> (Exodus 31:2-5)

Here are several keys I believe this passage gives to modern day artists:

• This is the only time I can see in the Old Testament where a man was "filled" with the Spirit of God! A thousand years before the cross of Christ, Pentecost, or the Book of Acts, God filled an artist with His Spirit in order to create a beautiful place for His Presence. It should tell us how deeply God values the relationship of partnering with artists!

- A work of art, the Tabernacle was a pattern of heaven, stamped with the mysteries of God, and this creative work was birthed by an artist who God specifically chose for the job and became spirit-filled so that he could create beauty. God entrusted the mysteries of heaven to an artist!

- The Tabernacle was filled with precious stones and jewels, including approximately one ton of gold ($12 million dollars) and about 3.5 tons of silver ($1,080,000), along with other precious stones and embroidered cloth. Even the priest's clothing was woven with thread made of pure gold. God is not stingy: He believes in supporting creative work that tells His story.

I also love how this passage says that God called this man by name and desired to create with him. The Lord knew exactly where to find such a man and pulled him out of the crowd at the right moment. He knows you too: God knows how to single you out of the crowd.

I believe God still looks for artists to fill with His Spirit in order to release a piece of heaven through art! He wants to create extravagant beauty with us, and birth art into the earth that His Presence can rest on. I believe He is calling artists to step into that place again! Hopefully these keys can help us get there:

- Let's redefine the word "perfect," and focus on completion and wholeness with Christ as our guide.
- Aim for excellence, but be patient with the process of maturing in our vision and skill.
- Looks for ways to invest extravagant beauty into our vision and invite people into a world of wonder.

LAUNCH THE VISION

ASK YOURSELF:

1) Have you ever wrestled with perfectionism? Describe.

_____

_____

_____

_____

_____

_____

2) Is God calling you to redefine this term?

_____

_____

_____

_____

_____

3) How does Christ aid us in Biblical completion?

_____

_____

_____

_____

_____

_____

4) Does the term "excellence" inspire or discourage you?

_____

_____

_____

_____

_____

_____

_____

5) What are some ways God may be calling you to grow in excellence?

_____

_____

_____

_____

_____

_____

6) Are there some ways He is telling you to relax and trust that He is enough?

_____

_____

_____

_____

_____

_____

7) Does the idea of "extravagant beauty" give you permission to explore your vision differently?

_____

_____

_____

_____

_____

_____

8) How do you feel about the Holy Spirit calling and choosing artists today?

_____

_____

_____

_____

_____

9) Would you like to ask the Holy Spirit to partner with you as a visionary/artist?

_____

_____

_____

_____

_____

_____

10) How is He asking you to partner with Him?

_____

_____

_____

_____

_____

_____

PART III

FIRE:

RELEASE YOUR VISION

Once you have tasted flight,
you will forever walk the earth with your eyes turned skyward,
for there you have been,
and there you will always long to return.
--Leonardo Di Vinci

LAUNCH THE VISION

CHAPTER SEVEN
LAUNCH

*"The greatest danger for most of us
is not that our aim is too high and we miss it,
but that it is too low and we reach it."*
– Michelangelo

There's something wonderful about holding your finished project in your hands, whether it's a book, film, music CD, or any other creative vision. The tingling sense of accomplishment and joy is indescribable, and the simple awareness that you've tapped into your destiny is such a valuable, precious thing. Let's face it: this place can also be a bit terrifying! We wonder, *Will anyone else see the value in this creation? How do I share it with the world?* Many artists have no idea how to market their work or start placing it into the hands of people who will love it. The last thing we need is a basement filled with boxes of product with no place to go, right? For artists, this can be one of the scariest places of the journey as we think, "what now?"

I'd like to dissolve some of these fears and give you some vision for Biblical promotion. After making lots of mistakes on this topic, I've made some discoveries that help launch a vision with joy and God's blessing. Even greater than the sense of creative accomplishment is hearing from people around the globe who have been moved by God through my creative project. For a complete stranger to connect with Jesus through my art is incredibly humbling and fulfilling, and even greater, to sense that my project is part of God's Kingdom and effectively producing fruit on the earth is overwhelming. This is one of the greatest joys of all, and it fuels my passion for the visionary journey like nothing else!

Jesus said,

By this My Father is glorified, that you bear much fruit;
so you will be My disciples.
John 15:8

The Father wants us to bring forth fruit! He loves when we radiate the expression of His love into the world and connect people with His heart. Art and media are amazing ways to do this! When we are a tool in His hand, many lives are touched and He receives glory.

So why is it so hard?! If the Father loves our expression and wants us to touch the world, how do we go about launching our vision to the place where this can happen? First, let's identify some of the fears that many of us struggle with, and work toward a godly perspective. By revealing these lies and seeing them from a different vantage point, the journey looks a bit less daunting.

SELF-PROMOTION

Scripture warns us about pride, becoming puffed up, and not thinking more highly of ourselves than we should, and most of us know that just talking about ourselves isn't going to sell our product anyway. On the other hand, we are also called to be good stewards of the talents He gives us and our creative work isn't going to help anyone if we're "hiding our light under a bushel." How do we balance God's calling on our lives with these two polarizing views? Many artists are stuck at this point of confusion.

Let's look at three points that enable us to balance both God's call to humility and shining brightly for Him. These steps will help us stay focused as we launch well.

Keeping a servant's heart. If you've truly crafted your vision out of care for others, to meet a need, or to express your soul to God, you'll recognize it's not really about you anyway. Your vision is serving the greater good, and so you can separate yourself from it and talk about the cause without constantly talking about yourself. In this way, you're serving others and the vision by simply representing it well with passion. If you're not passionate about your project, something is wrong! Figure out how to position your heart in the place of servant-hood as you talk about how your vision can help others.

Dedication. The first thing I do with a finished project is dedicate it to God. Super easy: I pray over my box of books and say, "God, I'm giving these to You! Use them for Your glory!" Then they don't belong to me anymore: they belong to His Kingdom! He is so faithful to place, price, and invest them in ways that bring forth fruit. If you've dedicated your vision to God, your heart continues to partner with Him in the launch!

Use your project to love others well. It's hard to be conceited when you really think others will be blessed by your vision, and you want them to enjoy it. If love is your goal, then is will help keep you on track. Also, if you're serious about giving your vision to God, He may call you to some platforms you feel unprepared for. However, if you simply focus on loving people in whatever situation arises, somehow all the pieces work out and God is glorified. You prove that you're part of His Kingdom by how well you love, both on a platform and behind the scenes.

FEAR OF MARKETING

Can't I just hire someone to market my product? I'm an artist and just want to focus on creativity! Unfortunately, the days of big record labels, producers who pay your way forward (and own you), and book publishers who do all your publicity are pretty much over. People with a platform generally have had to build it, at least at first. If you want your vision presented to people, you have to own it and do some of the marketing yourself. That's pretty much an awkward fact of the artistic world. In fact, as a newly published author, I know that big publishers are looking for authors who already have a platform and are working on their networking skills. If you expect someone to care about your vision enough to work hard at convincing people to love it, you need to start doing it yourself.

The hard part is that you HAVE to do it, but the good part is that you CAN do it! The power doesn't rest in the hands of some corporate hierarchy any longer, but in yours. You don't have to move to Hollywood or Nashville to get noticed and impact the world: you can do it from your backyard. We live in a generation that is more empowered with promotional tools than possibly at any other time in history, and taking this bull by the horns means there is so much room for God's Kingdom to expand through media. People are watching social media like never before, and that means they could be watching YOU. The internet is a mission field, and you can go without having to leave your living room! People are looking for beauty, uniqueness, and creativity, so if your vision fits that description, you will always have an audience.

So let's start figuring out a few things we can do well in the marketing world. We don't have to use all the social media platforms or constantly be tweeting to get attention. Like the shepherd boy David, we just need to pick up a few small stones to conquer this giant and have the courage to believe God will help us.

Key: marketing can be less about selling your product and more about finding more ways to share your heart. It can be fun and provide greater resources to share your passion along the way.

WHO'S WHO

If you want a list of "who's who" to launch your vision, let me give you a tip: you already have it. If you identify these tribes of people, you'll have the push you need to launch your vision. These are the three keys I use to launch my vision and market my resources.

WHO'S LISTENING?

If you're a visionary who is active in a community, you're probably already talking to people about your dreams and projects. People are naturally curious and drawn to passionate conversations, so hopefully you have some people who are aligned with your heart. There are two groups of people who you probably already have in your life: **doorkeepers and sheep.** Jesus defines these for us when He spoke about being the Good Shepherd,

To him the doorkeeper opens, and the sheep hear his voice;
and he calls his own sheep by name and leads them out.
And when he brings out his own sheep, he goes before them;

and the sheep follow him, for they know his voice.
John 10:3, 4

Your "sheep" are those who love your creative voice: they resonate with your music, art, or vision. They'll follow you on social media, come to your events, and buy your products. Sheep follow. They expect greatness from you, and they'll even back you on your journey. Your family, online followers, church and community can be sheep, because they already love you and what you carry.

"Doorkeepers" resonate with your voice, they'll invite you to the next level, and enable you to bring your sheep too. These are leaders who have influence and will help make a way for you. Mentors, pastors, magazines, TV, and bloggers can all be doorkeepers who can enable you to come up higher in influence.

It will take both sheep and doorkeepers to help you arrive at your creative destination, and it won't just be you arriving by yourself, because you'll be bringing them with you! Good leadership is knowing how to both partner with the doorkeepers and lead the sheep to a beautiful place. How do we do this? **The first step is to recognize who is already listening to you.** This is a great time to write a list of people who both love what you do and those doorkeepers in places of influence who could open some doors for you. Remember, start with what you have! Reach out to your community and ask for their support.

WHO IS READY?

One of the biggest pitfalls we get stuck in is to focus so much on our creative project and don't build a place for it to thrive when we finish. I've done this so many times! A creative project is like having a baby: you have to create a home for it before you birth it. A pregnant couple will not just focus on caring for the pregnancy! During that time they design a nursery, throw a baby shower, and build a community to welcome their child and help it grow. Anticipation grows in the community as they get excited and become invested in the arrival of the child. **Creating a project without investing in its release is like having a baby without preparing a home for it.**

The key to accomplishing this is to be preparing while you're "pregnant!" If you wait until your creative project is birthed in order to make a space for it, you will probably have to enjoy it all by yourself, and you'll have missed out on a lot of fun. Believe me, I've had times where I've been too scared to talk about my project until it's finished! I've wondered if I can actually survive the process, much less have something beautiful to offer. However, it's important to know that people want to believe in you if you give them a chance, and if you invite them into the process, you'll discover some great cheerleaders.

*"You can never go wrong by investing in communities
and the human beings within them."*
– Pam Moore

How do we do this? One way is to post lots of social media photos of the process. Invite people into your journey! People love to support those who are courageous enough to chase their dreams, and they become curious when you give them snapshots of what's coming. Be honest with your struggles, triumphs, and passion. Do live video blogs sharing your heart. Post photos and blogs that share even more of your passion: don't limit your passion to your project. Let your vision spill over in many ways, and people will get excited along with you. Just remember to communicate well and give people a way to respond by joining your social media platform or email list. By the time you're ready to birth your vision, you'll have some sheep that are excited to celebrate with you, and probably some doorkeepers who will help get the word out.

WHO'S WATCHING?

If you are posting publicly on social media, I guarantee you that people you don't even know are watching you. I've been one of those watching people: before inviting someone onto my TV show, I'll check their social media page and website. If they look professional and have a message like I'm looking for, I'll reach out with an invite. You never know who is watching your work and is ready to propel you to the next place of influence.

One time I pitched my TV shows to a network and was turned down by their committee. I had prayed long and hard for this opportunity, so it was disappointing when the door didn't open. A couple of years later, I was posting on social media about a new film I was working on and shared some of the still frames from the footage. For some reason (I'm still not sure how) I happened to be "friends" with their acquisitions person on Facebook. He saw me and messaged,

"How come you're not on our TV network? Let's talk."

I was in Alaska at the time and had to drive into town and sit in the grocery store's coffee bar to get a good phone signal. Over the phone, we put together a broadcast agreement, then he bypassed the committee and took it straight to the CEO of the network. I've been broadcasting with them ever since. You never know who is watching you! Sow your seed far and wide, because the harvest often comes from people watching that you don't even know about.

SURPRISES

I believe Biblical marketing is a way of partnering with God: it's a combination of you sowing into your community and God being faithful to bring the harvest. We all love when He does something sovereignly to bring instant success, but that would negate you as a partner! Our Father is so rich and powerful that He could snap His fingers and instantly bring you more success than you could imagine, but in my experience, He is far more interested in doing it with us than for us all the time. However, He is always working behind the scenes, and sometimes He lifts the curtain to remind us that He is up to more than we could imagine!

There's nothing like getting an email that reads,

"Just so you know, we are translating your TV program into Polish."

You just sit there and smile, thinking,

"Wow, my God is BIG!"

If you study the life of Jesus, you'll discover that He was constantly going ahead of His disciples and creating something beautiful for them.

"I'm going to prepare a place for you," He told them. He was always one step ahead, bringing them into a quiet place or knowing how to provide a feast in the wilderness for thousands of people.

In the voice of the Good Shepherd, he said,

And when he brings out his own sheep, he goes before them;
and the sheep follow him, for they know his voice.
John 10:3, 4

If we are truly following Christ with our art, we have to believe that He is going ahead of us to create opportunities and prepare the way. In this passage of scripture, the Greek phrase "goes before" is made up of two words meaning: *traverse or travel,* and *in front of.* Jesus is such a good leader that He goes in front of us to prepare the way for our creative journey.

I remember one day when I had just moved to a new city and was feeling both excited and alone. A new friend offered to give me a tour of the Christian TV network offices where she worked, so I met her in the cafeteria for lunch and then visited her office. On the way out, I picked up a pamphlet with a list of their programming and my mouth dropped open with shock. My TV show was listed on their schedule! I had never even spoken with these people before, and they were airing my show to thousands of people. Later I realized that I had signed with one of their affiliates, which is how they received my programming, so it opened up a great connection and I have since worked with them directly for several years. It was such an encouragement to know that the Lord had gone before me and was using my work to expand His Kingdom in ways I had no clue about!

CRUCIAL RELATIONSHIPS

Some of the people who will be influential in your creative journey may come alongside as you move forward. In fact, they may enter your world in the oddest, most beautiful of ways...

Flipping on the radio as I drove down a bumpy country road, a popular talk show with a husband and wife author duo caught my attention. As guests on the show, these relationship experts were sharing an intimate moment on their honeymoon when the young wife caught a glimpse of herself in the mirror and began to scornfully critique her body. The young husband took his wife in his arms and said,

"Anytime you need to know how beautiful you are, just

come to me and I will tell you. I'll be your mirror!"
Flashbulbs went off in my head as I thought, *That's what Jesus does to us! He is our mirror!* It sparked my creative juice and I penned the words to my song, *Mirror*:

> *Let me be your mirror*
> *Let me show you who you are*
> *We'll peel off those labels*
> *And we'll fix the fallen stars*
> *We'll crucify those photographs*
> *That never spoke you heart*
> *Cause I've seen through all the layers*
> *Just how beautiful you are*
> *It will all come clear*
> *If you let Me be your mirror*

It turned out to be a special song for my career and I used it in several films and projects. Seven years after writing the song, I was in Alaska and had the idea to shoot a music video with a few of my friends. (This was the third time I had filmed a music video to this song, because I kept having fresh vision for it.) We filmed in a gold mine, in a frigid stream of crystal-clear water, and under a waterfall. When it was done, I posted on social media and was contacted by Pam Farrel, an author and women's ministry leader.

"Your song would be great for my women's ministry!" she said. "Is it ok if I use it?"

A strange little thought pulled at my mind. *Who is this*

woman? I wondered. I did a quick internet surf and discovered that Bill and Pam Farrel were the talk show guests who had inspired the song seven years earlier. We spoke on the phone and I had the honor of thanking her for her ministry, and to share that her inspiring story was affecting people all over the world that she wasn't even aware of!

A few months later, I was working on a TV show that took me across country and Pam hosted me in her home as a guest for several months in California. She talked me into crafting a book proposal, and thanks to her help and several years of hard work, the book was picked up by a major publisher and the theme of beauty and identity was spread in a far greater way. Pam is still my mentor today and one of the most solid, faithful people I know. I consider her a role model and "spiritual mom" in so many ways, and she has been a constant source of wisdom in my life.

Others are watching our creative process, and if we simply create with excellence and share it, God will surprise us with the people He brings into our lives along the way!

LAUNCHING A BOOK

If you're an author, you're probably wondering about launching your book and whether to self-publish or pitch it to a publisher. I'll tell you my story and give you a few coaching tips that will help you figure out what could work best for you. There is no right or wrong answer, just a few options and good things to think about as you work toward your goals.

Self-publishing was daunting at first, but after my first several books, I found an amazing printer who could print on demand. After a few foolish mistakes along the way, I discovered that I could create as few or many books as I needed and have them on my doorstep in 10 days or less. I hired editors who looked for grammar and punctuation errors but didn't change my writing style, because I wanted to stay as true to the message as possible. I believed God had given me some special things to say, and preserving the anointing on that message was important to me. Creating a layout in a regular Word program was not too hard, and I could write a book or curriculum from start to finish and have it on my doorstep in a few months. It's been wonderful to print my books and keep all the profit from the sales which goes back to funding the ministry and buying my groceries.

After self-publishing 10 books myself, publishing *Finding Beautiful: Discovering Authentic Beauty Around the World* with Baker House Publishing was a major leap as I entered an entirely new world of working with a team to release a product and market it with a publishing house. That book was a three-year process, and I decided to look at the entire journey as an opportunity to grow as an author, so that no matter what happened, I'd be able to write better after working with people who knew a lot more about the industry than I did.

It began when my mentor introduced me to a literary

agent, and I signed with her for a year at no cost to me. (Good agents won't charge you a dime: they get paid from your commission if you get signed.) My agent was not only the real deal, but an excellent teacher. We worked on our book proposal for well over a year, which required 30 pages of in-depth research, info about my platform, and the first three chapters of the book. The process was difficult, but my agent was an excellent coach and we kept working and re-working the proposal until my best writing was pruned and sharpened. If not for my mentor and my agent, there is no way I'd have gotten signed!

Eventually she pitched the book, and Baker picked it up. Then began the long process of chatting with the new team, talking through the structure of the book, and writing the manuscript. Thanks to the long process of writing a structured proposal, the process was fairly straight forward. Because we had taken so much thought and strategy with the layout already, the writing was pretty easy and editing not too painful! They had several editors and proof readers work through the manuscript, and last minute I received a delightful e-mail:

"We've checked our budget, and we've decided to make the book hardcover with full-color photos!"

Little did Baker House know that this had been a dream I had believed unattainable! In fact, I had never even brought it up to them, because I simply thought it was impossible to have a publisher invest in a book with full-color photos, especially on your first book. However, they loved the stories and photos and really wanted to make it shine. We even worked together on the cover until everyone was pleased with it. (It took about eight photo shoots to craft a good cover photo!)

When I picked up my book from my P.O. Box, I nearly cried in the post office because it was such a culmination of hopes and dreams. The book was more beautiful than I could have imagined, represented my heart so well, and was a treasure I was so proud (and incredibly humbled) to share with the world. In all, my first published book has been an intense journey, but I am so pleased with the finished product. The Baker House team has been wonderful, and I'm honored to be on their roster of authors.

Self-Publishing Pros: You call all the shots, own your work, and no one dictates your message, method, or means. Your followers get exactly what they love from you. You can work at your own pace, whether that be three months or three years. There are no deadlines to cramp your style. You get paid for every sale.
Cons: You do everything yourself! There is no team to help hone and improve your craft, and your work is limited to you and your intentionality to bring people into the project. You will stay limited to your audience. There are no deadlines to push you forward.

Publishing Pros: You work with a team so the burden is not all on your shoulders. Your skills are refined if you stay teachable and ask good questions. The book becomes bigger than you and reaches farther than you. You get paid to write. Deadlines help you stay on task.

Cons: You still have to build your platform. (If you don't have a strong media platform, you probably won't get signed.) You have to be intentional about when to push back and when to comply. Don't fuss over small changes during the editing process: you're probably the only one who notices little things that are tweaked.

Launching our vision can come in many forms, but it will always have two things in common: representing Jesus well and communicating love to people. If you make those two things your focus, you can't go wrong! By the end of your launch, you'll have met some great people and grown closer with the friendships you already have. That's a great goal all by itself!

ASK YOURSELF:

1) Have you ever created something and not known how to share it?

_____

_____

_____

_____

_____

2) Do you fear "self-promotion?"

_____

_____

_____

_____

_____

3) Does the idea of "marketing with excellence" scare you?

_____

_____

_____

_____

_____

4) How does the Holy Spirit speak wisdom into these areas?

_____

_____

_____

_____

_____

_____

_____

5) On your "who's who" list: write some names of who's already listening.

_____

_____

_____

_____

_____

_____

6) Who are the doorkeepers who could be willing to help?

_____

_____

_____

_____

_____

_____

7) Is there anyone who can help mentor your creative process?

_____

_____

_____

_____

_____

_____

_____

8) Are there any new mentors who can speak wisdom and life into you?

_____

_____

_____

_____

_____

_____

9) (Just dreaming!) If you could choose anyone in the world to mentor you, who would that be?

_____

_____

_____

_____

_____

_____

_____

10) Is there anyone in your world you could treat to coffee and ask for coaching?

_____

_____

_____

_____

_____

_____

_____

CHAPTER EIGHT
MARKETING

*"You don't lead by pointing and telling people some place to go.
You lead by going to that place and making a case."*
– Ken Kesey

Marketing is not as hard as it used to be. Our culture loves vision and people get really excited about supporting people, and there are some very practical ways we can offer them what we carry. First, let's address some ideas that help prepare us for good marketing strategies. Often a helpful perspective will dispel some of the mystery around this topic and help us launch well.

PICKING UP THE TOOLS

Recently I had a dream that helped me understand God's strategy for marketing. It played out like a Narnian fantasy film, where I was journeying through a forest with a young princess and it was my job to defend her and get

157

her safely to the place of her coronation. Along the way, I met several attacks from goblins and war-like opponents determined to thwart my assignment. At one place, I found several beautifully carved swords and weapons near my path and realized they were placed there for me. However, I was very clumsy and they didn't do much good because I was simply untrained. The dream ended with me giving up on the journey because it felt impossible and trying very hard to wake up. Not a great ending!

Later that week I went to a media conference and attended sessions that described lots of new terms I had never been exposed to. Podcasts with RSS feeds and websites with SEO codes: the outcome of using these new tools could create beautiful results for God's Kingdom, but I felt overwhelmed at the thought of the learning curve required to use them. Also, I was attending under the title of *author* instead of *film producer* as I had in the past, which included many new relationships and a whole new side of the industry. It was a bit daunting and I had the thought, *Maybe this type of ministry is not for me!* It would be easier to check out than take the bull by the horns and embrace the next season of media ministry.

Putting my dream together with life circumstances, I realized that God was speaking about the calling He has entrusted me with. Many of us have a vision, dream, or calling on our lives and it's our job to bring that call to completion, like bringing a princess to her place of royalty on time. Just like a journey though uncharted territory, the way can seem unclear and even threatening, and we wish that promotion came easily. God places tools for us along the way, and we have the opportunity to learn how to use them, but sometimes we get overwhelmed and simply give up! I believe dreams from God help to identify and pinpoint our emotions, and even help us understand what NOT to do! We can change the ending of the dream and it doesn't have to play out that way in real life.

For many of us, marketing involves tools that we simply don't know how to use. However, this doesn't have to shut down our dreams, and promotion may be just around the corner!

FIRST IMPRESSIONS

Let's talk about presenting your project. For those of you who want to be taken seriously as an artist, author, or producer, let's remember that marketing is all about good communication. You know the saying, "you can't judge a book by it's cover," but the reality is that most people do. If you have a great book with a funky cover, it probably won't sell because people don't have time to read five chapters and decide if they like it before buying it. Marketing is about communicating your work in a way that speaks clearly and powerfully to the masses who need a strong first impression. To be honest, you have about 3 seconds to make them feel safe, invited, and curious about your vision.

To create a good first impression doesn't mean that we

need to be a super model or spend a lot of money to create a perfect image. Plenty of people in today's culture are really tired of "plastic" models and want to connect with normal people who have something to say. However, it's still important to put your best foot forward and connect in a meaningful way. Although God often does supernatural things to bring people across the right resource, people shouldn't need to be struck by lightning from heaven in order to pick up your product! Giving a good first impression is a healthy way to strike up a conversation, which is basically what you're asking your audience to do: engage with your heart through connecting with your product.

As Christians, it's important that we represent these practical areas well. Often we get all unbalanced in our vision and capitalize on presentation either too much or not at all. However, if we don't talk about it, we're selling ourselves short. I believe this is an area we can truly be "in the world and not of it," and use tools of this world without abusing it. If you and God both know that you have priorities in place, that's what matters, so building an image that represents you well is part of being responsible for your vision.

In the marketing world, you have about 3-10 seconds to make a first impression. That sounds daunting, but if you figure out what they're looking for, it's actually pretty easy to navigate. Whether on social media, a web site, or in person, people want to know the same things:

– You confidently carry something of value
– You are not needy or high-maintenance
– You will serve them well

Even before they every hear your vision, those are the common things most people look for. It has nothing to do with being a super-model or having a perfect life. As long as you qualify for those three things, you can get your foot in the door, and if you make it past that first impression, you'll often discover a willing ear who will take a moment to listen to your heart. With that idea in mind, here's a few tools I've found absolutely essential in getting past the "first impression" hurdle:

Business Card

Get a good one. Please do not get cards with a perforated edge! Go to VistaPrint.com and order something snazzy and classy. If someone wants to connect with you, this is an instant way of letting them know you are ready to follow up.

Head shots

Professional head shots are a MUST. If you want professional people to really take note, pictures from your phone or in the backyard are not going to cut it. A picture speaks a thousand words, so make sure your photos speak well of you! If you take responsibility to represent yourself nicely in this area, it lets people know that you care about presentation in a healthy way. A good head shot photo immediately says, *This person cares about their vision enough to step up to the next level and communicate well. They're investing in their vision, so they are probably a responsible human being.*

Website

Depending on the vision you are launching, a website is a huge help. Sometimes Facebook works by itself, but a website also provides an ongoing platform where you can update news, sell products, and create a little place where people can hang out. As a TV producer, I've approached many artists about being on my show and asked them if they have an online presence I can see. So many artists tell me,

"Well, my website needs updating..."

That phrase immediately tells me that they are not being intentional with their creative journey, and they haven't created a space for interested "doorkeepers" to check out what they are doing. If your website doesn't represent you well, you're not putting your best foot forward and you'll probably miss opportunities.

You don't have to spend a thousand dollars for a website. I create my own and host it for about $300 a year, and every time God is getting ready to promote my ministry to the next level, He prompts me to update my website to prepare for it. There are so many online site builders that are very easy to use and not too expensive. You can't go wrong with having a stellar website, so create one that works for you!

Social Media
Pick your top 2-4 social media platforms and use them regularly. If your creative vision has a product, go ahead and start a public Facebook page that people can follow. (I usually post daily on my page about a product for 30 days before a book/film/CD release.) This is a great way of communication that is easily accessible for people, and its free!

> *"Content is fire, social media is gasoline."*
> – Jay Baer

These things should to be in place BEFORE your vision launches. People will be looking at your online presence to find out more about you and what you are doing, so having them available is important to help people take you seriously. That may sound trite, but remember, it's all about communication. Are you communicating your vision well, or expecting complete strangers to invest their time and emotional energy in "getting to know you" in order to catch your vision? Part of serving people well is helping them access your vision in easy ways so they can enjoy it quickly. If you serve them well in this aspect of communication, you'll find many people willing to follow and stick with you.

Social media is also a great way to get feedback from your product. It's amazing how many connections and inspirations come from the comments below my posts.

Crafting an Image

This was not an easy concept for me to figure out! There was a time I had no interest in presentation or helping people connect with my vision, and this was reflected in how I dressed. When living in Deadwood, I wore jeans, T-shirts, and no make-up. After God called me to the ministry, I went to a thrift store, bought a plain, linen dress, and wore it to my speaking engagements for the first year of ministry. My thought process was this: *If God doesn't show up with His anointing, I am sunk anyway, so why try to impress anyone?* That sounded noble, but I can almost hear the Father chuckle as He watched me. My heart was right, but I wasn't being very approachable or gracious to those around me. Slowly, I began to find myself around women who knew how to dress, carried themselves with grace, and also loved Jesus! Without a word of correction from the Father, I began to find people who could help me dress for my body type and become a bit more appropriate and professional.

Crafting an image doesn't have to be something to be afraid of – it can be a lot of fun! It's just one more way to communicate the peace, beauty, and uniqueness that God has given you. So be yourself, be comfortable, and create a few tools that are gracious ways for people to connect with your heart and vision.

An "image" can be as simple as getting a good photographer to do a shoot with you and choosing a color scheme for your website that you like. It may mean crafting a logo that defines your workmanship. Seriously, it doesn't have to be a Hollywood super-star project. Just find some simple, consistent ways to help people know you are a safe, responsible person who is fun to be with.

Branding

For artists, crafting a brand can feel confining and like you're building a box to live in. We like to color outside the lines. This can be a difficulty, but it can also be a great way to tell your story and invite people into your world to encounter your heart. It requires self-awareness and figuring out how to translate your passion into something that others can wrap their brains around. You don't have to be defined by it: rather, it's just one more way of communication that helps serve the people who are embracing your vision. It can involve photos, colors, and creating a theme for your work. If you ask Him, God can give you some wild adventures in this area!

One of the most peculiar moments on my journey came when God brought provision for a photo shoot in an unlikely way. I had been working with a producer to record an EP and she had some very specific ways of getting things done, including talking me into hiring a photographer to shoot some cover photos. At the end of the shoot, we didn't like any of the photos, and it was rather disheartening. Around this time, I took a road trip to Colorado with a friend, and the first night we pulled into a hotel in the desert on the edge of some epic mountain scenery. A young couple was checking in next to us, and as we struck up a conversation about photography, it turned out that we had mutual friends. "Would you like to go off-roading with us?" they asked. "We were just about to take some photos of the sunset."

It was a tempting offer! Since my road trip companion was tired and ready to rest, she waved farewell as I grabbed my camera and jumped in their jeep. We sped over the rough terrain until we found an overlook, and my new friends turned off the ignition, pulled out an ipod and speakers, and began playing worship music that happened to be the exact album I had been listening to at home. Both of them were photographers, so they started snapping photos and posing me just for fun!

No make-up, tired after a long day of driving but exhilarated by the sheer adventure of it all, I just went along with the moment. The Colorado sunset was epic, and we snapped photos in "glory hour" which is favorite time of day for photographers. At the end of the shoot, they emailed me the photos. I used the beautiful shots for promo photos... and I never saw that couple again!

It was a crazy, beautiful moment where God saw my need and decided to meet it in a special way. I believe that He really does care about your brand and image, not it a self-serving way, but because it's such a great opportunity to do something beautiful for His glory! And it can be really fun.

MARKETING PRINCIPLES FROM JESUS

I was amazed to study the Gospels and discover that Jesus had some marketing techniques for His ministry.

Christ could have snapped His fingers and immediately called the world to attention, but instead He chose to start from the bottom as an unknown carpenter and build a following from scratch. During His anointed ministry, He never sat back and allowed miracles to gather a crowd: in fact, quite the opposite, He often hid His greatest miracles to avoid publicity. His organic means of communication still applies to us today and helps us realize it's really ok to work on getting a message out to people.

1. **Jesus went to centers of communication.** Synagogues were places of discussion, preaching, and hubs of social interaction within the community, and Jesus was often a guest speaker at these places. He didn't always wait for people to come to Him, but rather was actively speaking within the community. I think these places could represent modern-day churches, coffee shops, and other public venues.

2. **He needed a doorkeeper.** When Jesus was baptized by John the Baptist, he was recognizing the power of blessing and affirmation of other leaders. As a "doorkeeper," John knew that Jesus was coming, and released him into ministry. If Jesus did this, how much more do we need doorkeepers in our lives? Never be afraid to hang out with leaders and invite them into your project... they might even be waiting for you!

3. **He used what He had and borrowed things.** Jesus used what was close by for His ministry. He wasn't

afraid to ask for Peter's boat for a preaching platform, barrow a donkey to ride on, use a little boy's lunch, or ask for a coin to prove a point about Caesar. He even was buried in a borrowed tomb! He never relied completely on Himself or His power: He also brought people and their stuff on board in a healthy way to help spread the message.

4. **Jesus made time for followers.** Jesus didn't allow his followers to rule His life, but He did carve out time for them. Even when it was inconvenient, He spent extra time meeting their needs. (People are still valuable, whether on social media or in person. Make time for them!)

5. **Jesus branded Himself by using the name, Son of Man.** I love how He demonstrates the courage needed to give Himself a title! Rather than downplaying His role in ministry, He knew His identity well enough to tell people exactly what He stood for and helped them connect with who He was. In fact, He offered many angles for people to connect with Him: the Door, Good Shepherd, Light of the World, and Vine.

If you've ever felt like it's wrong to promote your message, think about the life of Jesus! He spent over three years preaching in public places and getting the word out about the Kingdom of God. There were times He was kicked out (and almost killed!) for preaching, but that doesn't mean God wasn't with Him. Other times, people questioned His motives and even suggested He was working for the devil. Because He was in step with God, the fear of what others thought didn't bother Him, even when the Pharisees accused Him of self-promotion by saying,

> *"All we have is your word on this.*
> *We need more than this to go on."*
> *John 8:13, The Message paraphrase*

He continued to be intentional about sharing the message, even though not everyone understood His heart, because it was the right time to launch His vision.

So, don't be afraid to step out into the marketing world! Not everyone will understand you or pat you on the back. Some people will doubt your motives or misunderstand your passion. It's ok- this happened to Jesus too. What's not ok is for you to ignore God's call on your life because of fear that you might mess it up. If you stay focused, you'll be able to hear the Holy Spirit as He helps you navigate, and if you get a little off, just get back on track and refocus. Keep moving forward and trust that He will guide!

MAXIMIZE YOUR PRODUCTS

One of the ways you can really expand your message is to make more than one product. For instance, I created the TV show *Radical Makeovers* by interviewing 50 women around the world and doing makeovers and photo shoots with them. Baker House Publishing released a book with

12 of those stories called *Finding Beautiful: Discovering Authentic Beauty Around the World*, and I went back and pulled those 12 stories and created a film to go along with the book. It didn't take a lot of extra work to create the film, and it's a great resource and helps get the message out! These three products were produced around one vision, and in the future, I might write a devotional to go with the theme too.

Get the idea? If your vision is big, craft your main idea and then think about other products people might also want. After producing the film *Spiritual Warfare 101* with sword fighters in Alaska, I realized I had more to say than what fit into the film, so I crafted a book to go along with it. People started asking if I had a leader's guide for youth, so I wrote a manual that people could use in their churches. If you're speaking on a topic that people want to know about, they may want more than a single product!

One more idea: after recording multiple worship songs, I created a DVD with music set to scenes of nature and scripture on the screen. It was a beautiful way people could soak in Scripture, and just another product that maximized the reach of my ministry. Think about your message and how to communicate it in several different ways!

MULTIPLY YOUR OUTLETS

Our media world is radically changing as the industry realizes that platforms are author/artist-driven rather than propelled by a publisher or label. Because of social media, visionaries have bypassed the huge gatekeepers of our times and have gathered their own followings. This is great, since we don't have to wait on the "big people" to give us access to platforms, but it also presents a challenge because crowds expect artists to still give them all the things a major publisher would. To do that, a visionary has to become comfortable with articulating their message in various forms.

One of the biggest things I can encourage artists is this: **your vision is bigger than one means of communication.** If you are passionate about a topic, you can write a book, sing a song, craft a blog, or paint a picture and still stay true to God's calling on your life. If we get stuck in one means of communicating that message, we'll often limit our audience. If you belong to Christ, you are more than an author or singer, you are a messenger who can communicate His message in multiple ways. Here's a few ideas:

Podcasts

For anyone who has ever dreamed about being on the radio, we live in a generation where you can literally create your own show and host it yourself on a podcast. Studies show that religious-themed podcasts are listened to more than any other topic, and it's a powerful way to get your message out. It's not too difficult and you can get a podcast hosting plan starting at $5 a month.

Self-publishing

After self-publishing 10 books, I can tell you that it's way easier than you might think. If your content is 25,000-50,000 words, you can create a great book that gives credibility to your ministry and offer a resource that people can take home with them. There are lots of print-on-demand sites that allow you to create as many or few as you need for just a couple of dollars per book. Other costs include editing/proofing, cover design, and layout. When complete, you simply save your document as a PDF, upload it to the website, and watch for your book to arrive in the mail! The company I use ships within 3 days.

Blogging

Blogging can be a great way to get your message out and provide people a way to interact with your vision. Recently, I realized I had over 52 composite art images and a message to go with each one, so I decided to start a weekly email devotional with a photo, scriptures, and I pasted it into the blog on my website and social media pages. Even if your blog doesn't get a lot of traffic right away, it's great for social media and is a good creative discipline for consistent writing.

Small Things

Another principle seen in the life of Jesus is that He wasn't driven by numbers. Moved by compassion, He stopped for the multitude or the single person-- it didn't matter which, as long as He was following the Father.

Watch for fruit, not numbers. If you have thousands of followers but no one's life is being changed or touched, then it will be a busy ministry but not necessarily a fruitful one. If you're having people tell you that God is impacting them through your creative work, than this something to get more excited about than numbers, because God is showing up.

I've known authors who have self-published 100,000 copies of books and given them all away by simply handing them to people as they strike up conversations during the day. I've created an entire music CD with one friend on my heart, thinking, *I just know she's going to love this!* Many people were blessed by the music, but that one friend wore out the CD and was touched and deeply ministered to by the message! Numbers are great, but the touch of the Holy Spirit is far more valuable than any amount of numbers, so watch to see where God is moving and rejoice when He does!

When encouraging a Hebrew king to build his vision, the Lord said that it was more important to build out of obedience to Him than to worry about whether the beginning stages looked impressive. He said,

This is the word of the Lord to Zerubbabel:
'Not by might nor by power, but by My Spirit,'
Says the Lord of hosts.
'Who are you, O great mountain?
Before Zerubbabel you shall become a plain!
And he shall bring forth the capstone

LAUNCH THE VISION

With shouts of "Grace, grace to it!...

For who has despised the day of small things?
Zechariah 4:6, 7, 10a

The biggest thing we can do is to be faithful. People come and go, but God is the one who establishes a ministry or creative project, and simply being trustworthy and faithful with what He gives you is enough! So don't be concerned if you don't have as big of a following as you hoped. Continue to be faithful and trust that He will bring the harvest in His time.

Marketing is a combination of you sowing into your community and God being faithful to bring the harvest. No matter how God leads you in this area, you'll be deeply humbled to watch His Spirit use you in mighty ways and grateful that He has allowed you to launch your vision and see it fly!

ASK YOURSELF:

1) What are some good, practical things to have in place before launching your product?

_____

_____

_____

_____

_____

_____

2) Do you have a professional, updated website?

_____

_____

_____

_____

_____

_____

3) Do you see social media as a place to communicate with others?

_____

_____

_____

_____

_____

4) Does the idea of "creating an image" feel like fun or just annoying?

_____

_____

_____

_____

_____

_____

_____

5) Branding: do you have a theme that fits your vision?

_____

_____

_____

_____

_____

_____

6) What are some marketing goals you'd like to have in place before launching?

_____

_____

_____

_____

_____

_____

7) Do you know people who can help make this happen? (Photographers/web designers, etc.)

_____

_____

_____

_____

_____

_____

8) Are there some skills you'd like to learn in this area?

_____

_____

_____

_____

_____

_____

9) Are there "places of communication" that would be interested in your vision?

_____

_____

_____

_____

_____

_____

10) Do you know any doorkeepers who would support what you do?

_____

_____

_____

_____

_____

_____

_____

CHAPTER NINE

CELEBRATE

"It's the greatest shot of adrenaline
to be doing what you have wanted to do so badly.
You almost feel like you could fly without a plane."
- Charles Lindbergh

At the end of every good journey, there's a great party. The Pevensies are crowned at Cair Paravel, Aragorn receives the throne, and Christian enters the Celestial City as angels rejoice. Your creative project is also a journey, so don't forget to script a celebration into your story! Eat some chocolate, throw a party, and enjoy the moment!

PARTIES
Jesus talked a lot about parties. He loved celebrating the accomplishments of God and His children. At the culmination of a quest, a long process, or an answered prayer, the characters in His parables threw huge parties

to rejoice. Celebrating is an opportunity to bring joy into your project!

- The prodigal son's father threw a party when he arrived home.
- After finding her lost silver coins, the woman called her neighbors to rejoice.
- In the parable of the talents, the servants were applauded for their faithfulness and told to, "enter into the joy of your lord."
- Jesus "rejoiced in spirit" when the apostles returned from a missions outreach.
- The angels in heaven rejoice when a sinner repents.
- At the end of the age, believers celebrate Christ's reign at the Marriage Supper of the Lamb and heaven throws a party.

CELEBRATING CREATION

When creating the world, the Master Artist, pausing after each day and pronouncing His creation "Good!" Finally, at the end of the sixth day, He took time to rest and enjoy what He had made. What a beautiful picture of artistic momentum is woven into the creation story!

And on the seventh day God
ended His work which He had done,
and He rested on the seventh day
from all His work which He had done.
Genesis 2:2

The word "rest" in this passage has the Hebrew meaning of: *repose, celebrate, rest.* If we embrace the creative pattern found in God's word, we'll discover that there's a time to party after we've finished our work!

Here's a few ways we can celebrate the birth of a creative project:

HOST A LAUNCH PARTY

As your creative project comes close to finishing, set a launch date for the release. Connect with a local church, bookstore, or coffee shop about hosting a release party, and even tell your local newspaper! You can serve refreshments, bring in live music, and give people a bit of the vision. If it's a film, show the movie and serve popcorn. If it's a book, do a book signing and speak on the topic, perhaps providing some fun, interactive ways that people can connect with the message. For a music CD, do a live concert! Of course, offer your product for sale and do a few giveaways during the night.

THROW AN ONLINE PARTY

Invite your Facebook friends to a live video where you talk about the vision and invite questions. Offer giveaways and do some fun promotions that bring others into the party. You can easily have a worldwide celebration on social media as you share your art!

GIVE GIFTS!

When my publisher launched my book *Finding Beautiful*, it felt like Christmas time. They kept sending me little boxes of beautiful postcards and handouts with the graphics from my book that I could give to others. They were so beautiful that each time I handed one out, I felt like I was giving a gift. It was a little embarrassing to keep getting these little packages, especially after self-publishing with my nose to the grindstone for several years! Sometimes we think the only beautiful thing we can create is our single project, but imagine what you can create with your project that will whet people's curiosity and give them a taste of it!

THE FATHER'S BLESSING

In the beginning of the book, we talked about how Jesus received the Father's blessing before launching His ministry. I love this, because it means we are never defined by what we accomplish, but only by our Father's love and blessing. The idea of living "from blessing to blessing" means that we start our creative journey with His blessing, rather than trying to achieve it through our work, and then have something beautiful to lay at His feet upon completion. When we launch our creative project, I believe there is another blessing at the end.

Jesus told the parable of the talents and offers a blessing to those who were faithful:

LAUNCH THE VISION

His lord said to him,
'Well done, good and faithful servant;
you were faithful over a few things,
I will make you ruler over many things.
Enter into the joy of your lord.'
Matthew 25:21

This verse has four parts to it which give powerful promises to the creative journey.

BLESSING
Well done, good and faithful servant;

A common interpretation of this verse is that we may hear this blessing when we get to heaven, but it also tells us about how the Lord deals with His people. The heart of this passage is a reference to the Lord's character, and how He blesses faithfulness and chooses to entrust His servants with more. I believe this is exactly what He does when we partner with Him and are faithful to release His creative visions into the earth.

One of the most beautiful moments of my creative journey is hearing the Father say, *Well done,* when I finish a project. I hear Him speak this every time I've created a project that He loves. It may come through a still, small voice to my heart, or through the words of a friend, or simply by hearing how people's lives have been changed as a result of the work. His blessing and promotion is released when we step into our destiny, listen to His heart, and release a creative vision on earth. Our Father is so good! Not only does He give a blessing before we start, but at the end of the finished product!

HONOR
you were faithful over a few things,

What better honor from the Lord could we receive than the acknowledgment that we have been faithful? Not perfect, flawless, or a superstar-- simply faithful. I don't know about you, but that's so beautiful to me! This verse also applauds those who have been faithful with "a few things," and the Greek word for this phrase means: *puny (in number, duration, or value), small, short.* God's kingdom is so different than ours: He loves using the foolish things to confound the wise, so He's not looking for those who think a lot of themselves. Instead, He wants so see if you'll be faithful with the small, even puny, things of this world. We can all do that!

PROMOTION
I will make you ruler over many things.

The Greek word for "many things" means: *much, abundant, great, plenteous.* The Lord entrusts us with more when we simply use what we have. Promotion comes from His hand, and He upgrades those who are faithful by giving them more. Jesus is a great cheerleader! He's never passive: He actively watches those who search after and seek Him. He values your endurance, tenacity, and the fact that you choose to follow Him. Any difficulty in the process does not go unnoticed. He does not take lightly those who are faithful!

JOY

Enter into the joy of your lord.

It's difficult to understand the joy of Jesus that's brought about by our faithfulness. If only we could understand that angels throw parties and Jesus gets excited when we step into our destiny! When we are faithful, it brings Him great delight because it brings the Father glory. When we are faithful to create with Him, others can taste and see that He is good. Our faithfulness brings Jesus great joy!

JOY IN OTHERS

There's not only joy in heaven when you create, but there's joy in the earth as you partner with the Lord! When I hear feedback from how people are touched by my art, sometimes I kind of melt! To me, the most beautiful parts of this process are: first, pleasing the Lord, and the second is being a part of His Kingdom plan. So many times, we'll never see how He uses our efforts this side of heaven, but when He gives us a glimpse, we know it's worth the labor! It could be as simple as a mom telling me,

"My three and five-year-old children have memorized your film about spiritual warfare, and I love that they are

learning positive character traits while being entertained!"
Believe me, there's nothing so humbling as listening to a three-year-old sing your song! Others write with life-changing stories of how God chose to show up through a piece of art or a song. When you start seeing the Spirit of God move through your art, there is nothing more humbling or beautiful than those moments!

I'm not always the best at following this piece of my own advice, but I'd encourage you to write these things down. What God does deserves to be written, and as you record how He shows up through your art, you'll have a beautiful track record of His work. Testimonies are precious, and they remind us what a privilege it is to give Jesus our gifts. The psalmist wrote:

Oh, taste and see that the Lord is good;
Blessed is the man who trusts in Him!
Psalm 34:8

One of the ways people taste and see the Lord's goodness may be through your art! Recording those testimonies is a way to celebrate what God has done.

COMPLIMENTS AND GRACE
If your project makes an impact, you'll have to decide what to do with the gratitude offered you. Compliments can go to our heads very quickly, especially if we're not used to our art being affirmed. How we respond to

praise is important, and it's an amazing opportunity to represent Jesus well!

How clearly I recall attending concerts as a teenager and looking up to the artists who had helped shape my world from their music. After the show, I often stood in the autograph line and tried to explain how deeply they had touched my life. My gushing, stumbling expressions weren't always very tactful, but I still clearly recall the artists' response. Those who said,

"All glory be to God," and quickly brushed me off, left me feeling foolish for trying to express my heart. In their effort to be humble, I felt brushed aside and unheard. But if an artist took time to listen to me, I was flying high for the next week! I remember one woman who responded to my accolades by saying,

"It means so much for you to share that with me," as she looked straight into my eyes for a moment before signing a fan poster. In that split moment, she taught me so much about owning your gift and responding with grace. In my feeble attempts to let her know how God had used her music in my life, I needed to know that my little heart mattered and that she cared – even for just a moment.

Your response to praise is just another opportunity to help people feel valued and loved by the Father. He cares about their hearts, and when they open up to share with you, it's a sweet way to offer affirmation to what He is doing. Obviously, healthy boundaries are necessary, but how you treat people is important to the Lord, so responding with grace and humility is just another way to love well.

Receiving accolades also offers another means of worship, because we can give the praise straight to Jesus in our heart! I love the quote by Holocaust survivor Corrie Ten Boom who became an influential speaker after WWII. Her life was such a miracle, and her book launched her into the limelight of doing huge events and receiving great applause from her fans. Instead of letting the response go to her head, she had a very gracious way of dealing with praise.

"When people come up and give me a compliment–
'Corrie, that was a good talk,' or
'Corrie, you were so brave,'
I take each remark as if it were a flower.
At the end of each day I lift up the bouquet of flowers
I have gathered throughout the day and say,
'Here you are, Lord, it is all Yours.'"

At the end of the day, we can either hold the compliments to ourselves and think about how great we are, or bring the Lord every bit of the glory and say, *Here you are, Lord, it is all Yours.* It's an amazing opportunity to continue the celebration on earth and in heaven as we launch our vision well! In this way, both the beginning and end of the journey revolve around the secret place of prayer. We take the seed of our vision to the Lord in the secret place, run back to Him to gleefully share the results, and we humbly offer Him all the glory and praise.

ENTER THE JOY

God was the one who initiated feasting in the Old Testament, and He actually commanded people to come together and joyfully feast several times a year. During the feasts, they remembered God's goodness, gave thanks, and made huge meals of food to enjoy together. Parties were commanded in Scripture! So, don't be afraid to invest in and enjoy this place of celebration! The opportunity to celebrate is something He invites us into, and we have the joy of partnering with Him in this way as we launch our vision!

Launch the Vision

ASK YOURSELF:

1 What are some ways you can celebrate your launch?

_____

_____

_____

_____

_____

_____

_____

2 How can you invite others into it?

_____

_____

_____

_____

_____

_____

3 What can you offer them as a gift?

_____

_____

_____

_____

_____

_____

4 Who are the people that will celebrate best with you?

_____

_____

_____

_____

_____

_____

5 What does it mean to create "from blessing to blessing?"

_____

_____

_____

_____

_____

_____

6 Do you feel the Father's pleasure when you create?

_____

_____

_____

_____

_____

_____

_____

7 If you could create a moment to celebrate with your Father, what would that look like?

_____

_____

_____

_____

_____

_____

_____

8 Do you believe that Jesus celebrates your faithfulness?

_____

_____

_____

_____

_____

_____

9 What do you see in the fact that God rested in the 7th day of His creation?

_____

_____

_____

_____

_____

_____

10 What are some ways to respond gracefully to compliments?

_____

_____

_____

_____

_____

_____

_____

CHAPTER TEN
CONCLUSION:
THE BEST STRATEGY

When the Queen says 'well done,' it means so much.
— Prince William

Recently I was at a large Christian media conference where thousands of "doorkeepers" met to discuss the recent trends and showcase the newest media forms in the industry. It was a high-energy week that was both exhilarating and grueling with the sheer amount of information presented. I was doing interviews for my publisher about my new book, and after the three-year process of pitching and penning the work, it was fun to see the finished product paying off.

One evening I kicked off my heels, threw on my tennis shoes, and went to see a film screening at the conference.

It was after business hours and I figured I didn't have to impress anyone, so I enjoyed the movie and stood in line afterwards to meet the producers. Next to me was a teenager, an aspiring actress with a bubbly personality who was excited about the film. As we chatted, my sisterly instincts kicked in and I asked if I could pray for her. Remembering myself as a teenager with big dreams, I could sense the Father's love as we bowed our heads in the middle of the auditorium. After we finished, I looked up to see tears on her face, and we had a "Jesus moment" of joy in the conference room.

Behind me, a smartly dressed blonde woman caught my attention.

"That was so sweet to see you pray over that girl," the stranger remarked. "What brings you to the conference?"

I had left all my promotional materials in my hotel room for the evening, so I simply told her about the vision of my book.

"I'm the CEO of a publishing company," she told me. "If you weren't signed to a publisher, I'd sign you myself."

I grinned and thanked her, laughing at the irony of the moment. *Lord, it would have been a lot easier to get a publishing deal this way, rather than spending 18 months crafting a book proposal,* I thought, *but that's not how You chose to do this.*

Instead of an easy deal, He had offered me an opportunity to launch my vision in a way that would help me grow as an author, but then He reminded me how simple it all can be when we just walk in love.

God is not bound to a single process: He knows how to help us best. Sometimes God may throw the doors open for you based on your heart's desire to love the people around you well. Other times He allows you to walk through a strategic process because the value is about who you become along the way. We see this in the words of King David, who, when offered an opportunity to receive land and build an altar for free, refused. Even though the landowner wanted to freely give him everything needed to worship God, David said:

"No, I insist on paying you for it.
I will not sacrifice to the Lord my God
burnt offerings that cost me nothing."
2 Samuel 24:24b NIV

David's attitude was greatly honored by the Lord, and the value he placed on the purchase price of worship was noted in heaven. Later, the site of this sacrifice became the location of the Jewish Temple, where the Shekinah glory of God rested as God honored that sacred space of dedication. As artists, we often want things to happen quickly, but David recognized the beauty of paying the price for something that was dedicated to God. If we want God to use our art, this kind of radical faith almost always plays a part in making it happen.

Sometimes the Lord may have you create a strategy to launch your vision, knowing that your faith and skill will grow in leaps and bounds during the journey. Or, a simple, pure act of love when we least expect it can turn the heart of a doorkeeper and bypass some of the process. The true strategy is humility, being faithful, and choosing to follow Jesus. The rest is up to Him, and it's beautiful either way!

LEARN MORE ABOUT REBECCA'S TV SHOWS, MUSIC, BOOKS, AND CREATIVE WORK!

Videos, photos, and artwork at:

WWW.REBECCAFRIEDLANDER.COM

LAUNCH THE VISION

Made in the USA
Monee, IL
02 January 2024

50934432R00121